CHARACTERS

WEINBERL
CHRISTOPHER
SONDERS
MARIE
ZANGLER
GERTRUD
BELGIAN FOREIGNER
MELCHIOR
HUPFER
PHILIPPINE
MADAME KNORR
MRS FISCHER
COACHMAN
WAITER ONE
WAITER TWO
GERMAN MAN
GERMAN WOMAN
SCOTS MAN
SCOTS WOMAN
CONSTABLE
LISETTE
MISS BLUMENBLATT
RAGAMUFFIN

PIPER, CITIZENS, WAITERS, CUSTOMERS, ETC.

On the Razzle was first performed on 1 September 1981 at the Royal Lyceum Theatre, Edinburgh as part of the 1981 Edinburgh International Festival, and opened to the press on 22 September 1981 at the Lyttelton Theatre. The cast included:

WEINBERL	Ray Brooks
CHRISTOPHER	Felicity Kendal
SONDERS	Barry McGinn
MARIE	Mary Chilton
ZANGLER	Dinsdale Landen
GERTRUD	Hilda Braid
A FOREIGNER	Paul Gregory
MELCHIOR	Michael Kitchen
HUPFER	John Challis
LIGHTNING	Thomas Henty and Timothy Hick
PHILIPPINE	Allyson Rees
MADAME KNORR	Rosemary McHale
FRAU FISCHER	Deborah Norton
COACHMAN	Harold Innocent
ITALIAN WAITER	John Challis
GERMAN COUPLE	Teresa Codling
	Clyde Gatell
SCOTTISH COUPLE	Greta Watson
	Andrew Cuthbert
SECOND WAITER	Philip Talbot
CONSTABLE	Alan Haywood
FRAULEIN BLUMENBLATT	Joan Hickson
LISETTE	Marianne Morley

Directed by Peter Wood
Designed by Carl Toms

On the Razzle

by Tom Stoppard

Adapted from
Einen Fux will er sich machen
by Johann Nestroy

A SAMUEL FRENCH ACTING EDITION

SAMUEL FRENCH

FOUNDED 1830

New York Hollywood London Toronto
SAMUELFRENCH.COM

ISBN **978-0-573-62000-3**   Printed in U.S.A.   **#17615**

INTRODUCTION

On the Razzle is an adaptation of *Einen Jux will er sich machen* by Johann Nestroy (1801–62), who flourished as a comic actor and playwright in Vienna during the 1840s and '50s. Nestroy wrote eighty-odd plays, a handful of which are still regularly performed in that city, while thirty or forty others have had at least one revival in the German-speaking theatre since the Second World War. It is still as a Viennese writing for Viennese that his fame survives, for his eccentric way with language amd his immersion in Viennese dialect gives partial truth to the assertion of one critic that Nestroy is 'untranslatable, even into German'.

This text is not, and could not be, labelled 'a translation'. All the main characters and most of the plot come from Nestroy but almost none of the dialogue attempts to offer a translation of what Nestroy wrote. My method might be compared to cross-country hiking with map and compass, where one takes a bearing on the next landmark and picks one's own way towards it.

Nestroy's way was satirical and verbally outrageous and often turned on a local reference. He also liked to include comic songs between scenes. *On the Razzle* makes no use of dialect, ignores period flavour in dialogue, and has no songs. It is still set in Vienna (though about fifty years later than *Einen Jux*) but not essentially so. The two essentials which this play takes from the original are, firstly, the almost mythic tale of two country mice escaping to town for a day of illicit freedom, adventure, mishap and narrow escapes from discovery; and, secondly, the prime concern to make the tale as comic an entertainment as possible.

Having no German I am indebted to Neville and Stephen Plaice who prepared a close literal translation for me at the request of the National Theatre (and who suggested the title). To Peter Wood, who directed the National Theatre production, is owed the idea of bringing a new version of *Einen Jux* from the Danube to the South Bank.

I say 'new' version because there is already a celebrated old one, Thornton Wilder's *The Matchmaker*. It is not widely known—I didn't know it myself—that Wilder's play and (hence *Hello Dolly!* as well) is an adaptation of *Einen Jux*. When I discovered this I turned to other Nestroy plays thinking that perhaps in bringing a play from this almost unknown comic master into the English theatre I should take a path less famously trod, but I soon returned to *Jux* (its title contracting as affection grew). Firstly, this was the play which Peter Wood most wanted to do, attracted by the mythic quality mentioned above. Secondly, Wilder's temperament, which serves *The Matchmaker* so well, made gentler and more dignified use of the original than I intended, while, furthermore, his adaptation of the plot was rather more free than anything I had in mind. For example Dolly Levi, the matchmaker of the title, is Wilder's own invention.

So I offer myself the hope that the differences between the two are at least as great as the similarities, and that *On the Razzle*, if not an absolutely essential addition to the canon of adaptations in English from *Einen Jux will er sich machen*, is at least a welcome one.

TOM STOPPARD

AUTHOR'S NOTE

Although this text, like the first edition, is in two acts, the original production was done with two intermissions, the middle act beginning with 'The Journey to Vienna' and ending with the Restaurant Scene.

ACT ONE

Zangler's shop
In which customers are served with great panache by WEINBERL *and*
CHRISTOPHER. MARIE *is the cashier in a gilded cage. Old-fashioned*
spring-loaded canisters travel on wires between the cage and the
counters. A chute delivers a large sack of flour from up above to a
position behind WEINBERL'S *counter. There is a trap door to a cellar.*
SONDERS, *incognito, is among the customers. A town clock chimes the*
hour. Customers are being ushered out by CHRISTOPHER. SONDERS
remains. Shop closing for lunch.

Zangler's room can occupy the stage with the shop, the action moving
between the two.
ZANGLER *and* GERTRUD. ZANGLER *is usually worked up, as now.*
GERTRUD *never is.*
ZANGLER: My tailor has let me down again.
GERTRUD: Yes, I can see.
ZANGLER: No, you damned well can't. I'm referring to my new
    uniform which hasn't arrived yet, and today is the grand
    annual parade with the massed bands of the Sporting and
    Benevolent Societies of the Grocers' Company. It's enough to
    make one burst a bratwurst. I'll feel such a fool ... There I'll be,
    president-elect and honorary whipper-in of the Friends of the
    Opera Fur and Feather Club, three times winner of the Johann
    Strauss Memorial Shield for duck-shooting, and I'll have to
    appear before the public in my old uniform. Perhaps I'd better
    not go out at all. That fortune-hunter Sonders is after my ward.
GERTRUD: My word.
ZANGLER: My ward! I won't rest easy until Marie is safely out of
    his reach. Now, don't forget, Marie's luggage is to be sent
    ahead to my sister-in-law's, Miss Blumenblatt at

twenty-three Carlstrasse.

GERTRUD: Miss Blumenblatt's.

ZANGLER: What is the address?

GERTRUD: Twenty-three Carlstrasse.

ZANGLER: What is it?

GERTRUD: Twenty-three Carlstrasse.

ZANGLER: Very well. Marie can stay with her until Sonders finds some other innocent girl to pursue, and furthermore it will stop the little slut from chasing after *him*. I'm damned sure they're sending messages to each other but I can't work out how they're doing it.

(*Zing! In the shop—now closed—a cash-canister zings along the wire to* MARIE *in her gilded cage.*)

Zangler's shop

The shop is closed. WEINBERL *and* CHRISTOPHER *are absent.* SONDERS, *half hidden, has sent the canister.* ZANGLER *is on to him.*

ZANGLER: Sonders!

MARIE: Uncle!

SONDERS: Herr Zangler!

ZANGLER: Unhand my foot, sir!

SONDERS: I love your niece!

ZANGLER: (*Outraged*) My knees, sir? (*Mollified*) Oh, my *niece*. (*Outraged*) Well, my niece and I are not to be prised apart so easily, and nor are hers, I hope I make my meaning clear?

SONDERS: Marie must be mine!

ZANGLER: Never! She is a star out of thy firmament, Sonders! I am a Zangler, provision merchant to the beau-monde, top board for the Cheesemongers and number three in the Small Bore Club.

SONDERS: Only three?

ZANGLER: Do you suppose I'd let my airedale be hounded up hill and—my heiress be mounted up hill and bank by a truffle-hound—be trifled with and hounded by a mountebank?! Not for all the tea in China! Well, I might

12

for all the tea in China, or the rice—no, that's ridiculous—
the preserved ginger then—no, let's say half the tea, the
ginger, a shipment of shark-fin soup double-discounted just
to take it off your hands—

SONDERS: All you think about is money!

ZANGLER: All I think about *is* money! As far as I'm concerned
any man who interferes with my Marie might as well have
his hand in my till!

SONDERS: I make no secret of the fact that I am not the *éminence
grise* of Oriental trade, but I have expectations, and no
outstanding debts.

(*A man, a* FOREIGNER, *visible in the street, starts knocking on
the shop door.* MARIE *has emerged from her cage and goes to
deal with it.*)

FOREIGNER: Grus Grott! (*He enters and shakes hands all round.*)

ZANGLER: We're closed for lunch. What expectations?

FOREIGNER: Enshuldigen!

ZANGLER: Closed!

FOREIGNER: Mein heren! Ich nicht ein customer . . .

ZANGLER: What did he say?

MARIE: I don't know, Uncle, I think he's a foreigner.

FOREIGNER: Gut morgen—geshstattensie—bitte shorn—danke
shorn . . .

ZANGLER: We're closed! Open two o'clock!

FOREIGNER: Ich comen looken finden Herr Sonders.

ZANGLER: Here! Sonders!

FOREIGNER: Herr Sonders?

ZANGLER: No, *there* Sonders.

FOREIGNER: Herr Sonders? Ich haben ein document.

ZANGLER: He's a creditor!

FOREIGNER: Herr Sonders!

ZANGLER: No debts, eh?

FOREIGNER: Ja—dett!—

SONDERS: Nein, nein—I'm busy. Comen backen in the morgen.

(SONDERS *ushers the* FOREIGNER *out of the shop. The* FOREIGNER
*is in fact a legal messenger who has come from Belgium to
announce the death of* SONDERS's *rich aunt. He succeeds in this
endeavour at the end of the play.*)

ZANGLER: I thought you said you had no debts!

SONDERS: No outstanding debts—run-of-the-mill debts I may
have. I probably overlooked my hatter, who is a bit short.
But as for my expectations, Herr Zangler, I have the
honour to inform you that I have a rich aunt in Brussels.
ZANGLER: A rich aunt in Brussels! I reel, I totter, I am routed
from the field! A rich aunt in Brussels—I'm standing here
with my buttons undone and he has a rich aunt in Brussels.
SONDERS: She's going to leave me all her money.
ZANGLER: When is that?
SONDERS: When she's dead, of course.
ZANGLER: Listen, I know Brussels. Your auntie will be sitting up
in bed in a lace cap when Belgium produces a composer.
SONDERS: I hope so because while she lives I know she'll make
me a liberal allowance.
ZANGLER: A liberal allowance!? How much is that in Brussels?
I'm afraid I never do business on the basis of grandiloquent
coinage, and in the lexicon of the false prospectus 'a liberal
allowance' is the alpha and oh my God, how many times
do I have to tell you?—I will not allow my ward to go off
and marry abroad.
SONDERS: Then I'll stay here and marry her, if that's your
wont.
ZANGLER: And meanwhile in Brussels your inheritance will be
eaten to the bone by codicils letting my wont wait upon her
will like the poor cat with the haddock.
SONDERS: The what?
ZANGLER: Look to the aunt! Don't waste your time mooning and
skulking around my emporium—I'm sending Marie away to
a secret address where you will never find her, search how
you will.
(*To* GERTRUD *who has entered with* ZANGLER's *old uniform*.)
What is it?!
GERTRUD: Twenty-three Carlstrasse, Miss Blumenblatt's.
SONDERS: Twenty-three Carlstrasse . . .! Miss Blumenblatt's!
ZANGLER: (*Spluttering*) You old—you stupid—
GERTRUD: Should I let Marie have the new travelling case?
ZANGLER: —old baggage!
GERTRUD: *Not* the new travelling case . . .
SONDERS: (*Leaving*) My humble respects . . .

GERTRUD: Here is your old uniform. And the new servant has
    arrived.
SONDERS: Your servant, ma'am!
GERTRUD: His.
    (SONDERS *goes.*)
ZANGLER: You prattling old fool, who asked you to open your
    big mouth?
GERTRUD: You're upset. I can tell.
ZANGLER: Where is Marie?
GERTRUD: She's upstairs trying on her Scottish travelling outfit
    you got her cheap from your fancy.
ZANGLER: My fancy? My fiancée! A respectable widow and the
    Madame of 'Madame Knorr's Fashion House'.
GERTRUD: I thought as much—so it's a betrothal.
ZANGLER: No it isn't, damn your nerve, it's a hat and coat shop!
    Now get out and send in the new servant. And don't let
    Marie out of your sight. If she and Sonders exchange so
    much as a glance while I'm gone I'll put you on cabbage-
    water till you can pass it back into the soup-pot without
    knowing the difference.
    (*Exit* GERTRUD.)
    This place is beginning to lose its chic for me. I bestride
    the mercantile trade of this parish like a colossus, and run a
    bachelor establishment second to none as far as the eye can
    see, and I'm surrounded by village idiots and nincompetent
    poops of every stripe. It's an uphill struggle trying to instil
    a little tone into this place.
    (*There is a knock on the door.*)
    Entrez!
    (*There is a knock on the door.*)
    (*Furiously*) Come in!
    (*Enter* MELCHIOR.)
MELCHIOR: Excuse me, are you the shopkeeper, my lord?
ZANGLER: You do me too much honour and not enough. I am
    Herr Zangler, purveyor of high-class provisions.
MELCHIOR: I understand you are in desperate need of a servant.
ZANGLER: You understand wrong. There's no shortage of rogues
    like you, only of masters like me to give them gainful
    employment.

MELCHIOR: That's classic. And very true. A good servant will keep for years, while masters like you are being ruined every day. How's business by the way?—highly provisional, I trust?

ZANGLER: You strike me as rather impertinent.

MELCHIOR: I was just talking shop. Please disregard it as the inexperience of blushful youth, as the poet said.

ZANGLER: Do you have a reference?

MELCHIOR: No, I just read it somewhere.

ZANGLER: Have you got a testimonial?

MELCHIOR: (*Producing a tattered paper*) I have, sir. And it's a classic, if I say so myself.

ZANGLER: Do you have any experience in the field of mixed merchandise?

MELCHIOR: Definitely, I'm always mixing it.

ZANGLER: Well, I must say, I have never seen a testimonial like it.

MELCHIOR: It's just a bit creased, that's all.

ZANGLER: 'Honest, industrious, enterprising, intelligent, responsible, cheerful, imaginative, witty, well-spoken, modest, in a word classic . . .'

MELCHIOR: When do you want me to start?

ZANGLER: Just a moment, aren't you forgetting the interview?

MELCHIOR: So I am—how much are you paying?

ZANGLER: Six guilders a week, including laundry.

MELCHIOR: I don't do laundry.

ZANGLER: I mean the housekeeper will wash your shirts.

MELCHIOR: That's classic. I like to be clean.

ZANGLER: And board, of course.

MELCHIOR: Clean and bored.

ZANGLER: And lodging.

MELCHIOR: Clean and bored and lodging—

ZANGLER: All included.

MELCHIOR: Ah, board and lodging. How about sharing a bed?

ZANGLER: I won't countenance immorality.

MELCHIOR: Own bed. As for the board, at my last place it was groaning fit to bust, the neighbours used to bang on the walls.

ZANGLER: I assure you, no one goes hungry here: soup, beef, pudding, all the trimmings.

MELCHIOR: Classic. I always have coffee with my breakfast.

ZANGLER: It has never been the custom here for the servant to have coffee.

MELCHIOR: You wouldn't like me to drink liquor from the stock.

ZANGLER: Certainly not.

MELCHIOR: I should prefer to avoid the temptation.

ZANGLER: I'm glad to hear it.

MELCHIOR: Agreed, then.

ZANGLER: What? Well, if you do a good job . . . coffee then.

MELCHIOR: From the pot?

ZANGLER: Ad liberandum.

MELCHIOR: Is that yes or no?

ZANGLER: Yes.

MELCHIOR: Sounds classic. Was there anything else you wanted to ask me?

ZANGLER: No . . . I don't think so.

MELCHIOR: Well, that seems satisfactory. You won't regret this, sir—I have always parted with my employers on the best of terms.

ZANGLER: You have never been sacked?

MELCHIOR: Technically, yes, but only after I have let it be known by subtle neglect of my duties that the job has run its course.

ZANGLER: That's very considerate.

MELCHIOR: I don't like to cause offence by giving notice—in a servant it looks presumptuous.

ZANGLER: That shows modesty.

MELCHIOR: Your humble servant, sir.

ZANGLER: Yes, all right.

MELCHIOR: Classic!

ZANGLER: Only you'll have to stop using that word. It's stupid.

MELCHIOR: There's nothing stupid about the word. It's just the way some people use it without discrimination.

ZANGLER: Do they?

MELCHIOR: Oh yes. It's absolutely classic. What are my duties?

ZANGLER: Your duties are the duties of a servant. To begin with you can make my old uniform look like new—and if that tailor shows his face tell him to go to hell.

(*Enter tailor,* HUPFER. HUPFER *brings with him* ZANGLER's *new uniform on a tailor's dummy. The complete rig-out includes a ridiculous hat with feathers etc., polished riding boots with monstrous shining and very audible spurs, and the uniform itself which is top heavy with gold buttons and braid etc. Leather strapping supports holsters for knife, gun, sword . . . The general effect is sporting and musical. The new uniform is brighter than the old, which is bright. The tailor is only responsible for the clothes. The rest of the stuff is already in the room.*)

HUPFER: Here we are—the masterpiece is ready.

ZANGLER: You managed it, my dear Hupfer! In the nick of time.

MELCHIOR: Go to hell.

ZANGLER: Shut up!

MELCHIOR: (*To the dummy*) Shut up!

HUPFER: Well, with the help of two journeyman tailors I have done the impossible—let me help you into it.

MELCHIOR: Too small.

HUPFER: (*Reacts to* MELCHIOR) I see you have a new servant, Herr Zangler.

ZANGLER: (*Cheerfully*) Oh yes. I woke up this morning feeling like a new man. So I got one.

HUPFER: Trousers.

MELCHIOR: Too tight.

HUPFER (*Wary distaste*) He's a personal servant, is he?

ZANGLER: Yes, he is a bit, but I like to give youth a chance and then I like to kick it down the stairs if it doesn't watch its lip.

MELCHIOR: I worked for a tailor once. I cooked his goose for him.

HUPFER: There we are.

MELCHIOR: Everything went well until I got confused and goosed his cook.

ZANGLER: Pay attention. You may learn something.

MELCHIOR: After that he got a valet stand.

ZANGLER: You'll see how a trouser should fit . . . except it's a bit tight isn't it?

(*It is more than a bit tight.*)

HUPFER: Snug.

ZANGLER: Snug? I'd be in trouble if I knelt down. I'm thinking of my nuptials.

HUPFER: It's the pressing.

ZANGLER: Exactly. I don't *want* them pressed.

HUPFER: Try the tunic.

ZANGLER: I like the frogging.

HUPFER: Can we please keep our minds on the tunic. Now let me help you.

ZANGLER: It's somewhat constricted, surely.

HUPFER: That's the style.

ZANGLER: But it's cutting me under the arms, the buttons will fly off when I sit down, and I can't breathe.

HUPFER: It's a uniform, it is not supposed to be a nightshirt.

ZANGLER: I don't understand it. You took my measurements.

MELCHIOR: Well that explains it. If God had been a tailor there'd be two and a half feet to the yard and the world would look like a three-cornered hat . . .

ZANGLER: And it's a day late.

MELCHIOR: And it would have been a day late. We'd all be on an eight-day week.

ZANGLER: Shut up.

MELCHIOR: (*To the dummy*) Shut up.

ZANGLER: I suppose it will have to do, at a pinch. How do I look?

MELCHIOR: I'd rather not say.

ZANGLER: I order you—how do I look?

MELCHIOR: Classic.

ZANGLER: Shut up!

MELCHIOR: (*To* HUPFER) Shut up!

HUPFER: You dare to let your servant speak to me like that?

MELCHIOR: In the livery of the Zanglers I am no man's minion.

ZANGLER: That's well said. What's your name?

MELCHIOR: Melchior.

ZANGLER: Melchior, throw this man out.

HUPFER: Don't touch me! You, sir, received your measurements from nature. The tailor's art is to interpret them to your best advantage, and move the buttons later. My humble respects. I will leave my bill.

MELCHIOR: (*Thrusting the dummy at* HUPFER) Oh no you won't— you'll take him with you!

(*Exit* HUPFER *with dummy.*)

What should I do next?

ZANGLER: There's a coach leaving for town in five minutes. I want you to be on it.

MELCHIOR: It's been a pleasure. I usually get a week's money.

ZANGLER: No, no, my dear fellow, I want you to go to Vienna and engage a private room at the Black and White Chop House. Order a good dinner for two and wait for me there.

MELCHIOR: Dinner for two, wait for you there.

ZANGLER: Tell them it's a celebration—foaming tankards—cold meats—pickles—potato salad—plum dumplings . . .

MELCHIOR: You'll spoil me.

ZANGLER: It's not for you. I'm entertaining my fiancée to a birthday dinner.

MELCHIOR: A previous engagement? My congratulations, Herr Zangler.

ZANGLER: Thank you. She's the Madame of Madame Knorr's Fashion House. You may know it.

MELCHIOR: No, but I think I know the piano player.

ZANGLER: It's a hat shop in Annagasse. Of course she's a millineress in her own right.

MELCHIOR: Enough said. And the shop on top.

ZANGLER: No, she's on top of the shop. What are you talking about?

MELCHIOR: I don't know.

ZANGLER: I'm going to take her to dinner and name the day. You can expect me after the parade.

MELCHIOR: Are we travelling together?

ZANGLER: No, I can't be in a hurry, I'm having trouble with my niece.

MELCHIOR: It's the uniform.

ZANGLER: No, it's the Casanova incarnate. Marie is very vulnerable. If she so much as sets foot outside the door she's going to catch it from me.

MELCHIOR: How long have you had it?

ZANGLER: No. I mean the Don Juan.

MELCHIOR: Has he had it?

ZANGLER: I don't think so. She's in her room trying on her Scottish get-up.

MELCHIOR: I'll work it out later.

ZANGLER: After all I am her uncle.

MELCHIOR: I've worked it out.

ZANGLER: I sent him packing with a flea in his ointment.

MELCHIOR: I think I saw him leave.

ZANGLER: Now here's some money to catch the coach.

MELCHIOR: Can't I meet the rest of your staff?

ZANGLER: There isn't time. Do you understand my requirements?

MELCHIOR: Perfectly.

ZANGLER: Repeat them.

MELCHIOR: Catch the coach—go straight to the Imperial Gardens Café—private dinner for two, champagne on ice . . .

ZANGLER: No—no—no—the Black and White Chop House!

MELCHIOR: Sir, I beg you to consider. Madame Knorr is a woman of the world, sophisticated, dressed to the nines with a hat to knock your eye out and an eye to knock your hat off. You want to wine her, dine her and name the day. Now does that suggest to you a foaming tankard and a plate of cold cuts in the old Black and White?

ZANGLER: (*Slightly puzzled*) Yes it does. What are you getting at?

MELCHIOR: Madame Knorr is not just another hausfrau. Fashion is her middle name.

ZANGLER: More or less. Knorr Fashion House. I think I see what you mean . . . The Imperial Gardens Café is a fashionable place, is it?

MELCHIOR: It's the only place for the quality at the moment.

ZANGLER: The quality . . . Are you sure it is quite refined?

MELCHIOR: Refined?! The ploughman's lunch is six oysters and a crème de menthe frappé.

ZANGLER: I see . . . well, perhaps just this once.

MELCHIOR: Leave it to me, sir—champagne—lobster—roast fowl—birthday cake—

ZANGLER: Pickles—dumplings—

MELCHIOR: And to finish off, to get her in the mood—

ZANGLER: Perhaps we should have—

MELCHIOR: ⎫
ZANGLER: ⎭ (*Together*) A nice bottle of the hard stuff.

MELCHIOR: (*Leaving*) Schnapps!

(*Coach horn.* ZANGLER *now puts on the rest of his outfit, boots, hat, etc.*)

ZANGLER: Well, that seems all right. Just the ticket. First class. Why do I have a sense of impending disaster? (*He reflects.*) Sonders is after my niece and has discovered the secret address where I am sending her to the safe keeping of my sister-in-law Miss Blumenblatt, who has never laid eyes on him, or, for that matter, on Marie either since she was a baby—while I have to leave my business in the charge of my assistant and an apprentice, and follow my new servant, whom I haven't had time to introduce to anyone, to town to join the parade and take my fiancée to dinner in a fashionable restaurant in a uniform I can't sit down in.

One false move and we could have a farce on our hands. (*He exits.*)

Zangler's shop
The shop is closed for lunch. WEINBERL *occupies it like a gentleman of leisure. He is writing a letter at the counter. He has a cigar and a glass of wine.* CHRISTOPHER *is at the door leading to the rest of the house. He is holding a broom, the Cinderella-type of broom, not a yard broom.*
CHRISTOPHER: He's gone.
(*He joins* WEINBERL *and is offered a glass. There is also a jar of rollmops to hand.*)
Ah, thank you, Mr Weinberl.
(WEINBERL *continues to write. At* CHRISTOPHER'*s position on the counter there is a stack of torn pages from newspapers used here for wrapping purposes.* CHRISTOPHER *leans on the stack, reading the top page.*)
Aha, I thought so . . . cocoa is up six points.
WEINBERL: (*Without looking up*) When was that?
CHRISTOPHER: (*Examining the top of the page*) Week before last.
(WEINBERL *signs his letter and blots it.*)
WEINBERL: Does it ever occur to you, Christopher, that we're the backbone of this country?
CHRISTOPHER: You and me, Mr Weinberl?
WEINBERL: The merchant class.
CHRISTOPHER: Ah yes.
WEINBERL: The backbone of the country. The very vertebrae of

continental stability. From coccyx to clavicle—from the
Carpathians to . . . where you will . . .

CHRISTOPHER: The toe-nails . . .

WEINBERL: . . . the Tyrol, from Austro to breakfast, and
Hungaria to lights out, the merchant class is the backbone
of the empire on which the sun shines out of our doings;
do you ever say that to yourself?

CHRISTOPHER: Not in so many words, Mr Weinberl.

WEINBERL (*Pulling* CHRISTOPHER's *forelock*) Well you should.
What is it after all that distinguishes man from beast?

CHRISTOPHER: Not a lot, Mr Weinberl.

WEINBERL: Trade.

CHRISTOPHER: I was thinking that.

WEINBERL: What would we be without trade?

CHRISTOPHER: Closed, Mr Weinberl.

WEINBERL: That's it. The shutters would go up on civilization
as we know it. It's the merchant class that holds everything
together. Uniting the deep-sea fisherman and the village
maiden over a pickled herring on a mahogany counter . . .

CHRISTOPHER: You've put me right off me rollmop.

(*He has been eating one.*)

WEINBERL: . . . uniting the hovels of Havana and the House of
Hanover over a box of hand-rolled cigars, and the matchgirl
and the church warden in the fall of a lucifer. The pearl fisher
and the courtesan are joined at the neck by the merchant
class. We are the brokers between invention and necessity,
balancing supply and demand on the knife edge of profit
and loss. I give you—the merchant class!

CHRISTOPHER: The merchant class!

(*They toast.*)

WEINBERL: We know good times and we know bad. Sometimes
trade stumbles on its march. The great machine seems to
hesitate, the whirling cogwheels and reciprocating pistons
disengage, an unearthly silence descends upon the mercantile
world . . . We sit here idly twisting paper into cones, flicking
a duster over piles of preserved figs and pyramids of
uncertain dates, swatting flies like wanton gods off the
north face of the Emmental, and gazing into the street.
   And then suddenly with a great roar the engine bursts

into life, and the teeming world of commerce is upon us! Someone wants a pound of coffee, someone else an ounce of capers, *he* wants smoked eel, *she* wants lemons, a skivvy wants rosewater, a fat lady wants butter, but a skinny one wants whalebones, the curate comes for a candy stick, the bailiff roars for a bottle of brandy, and there's a Gadarene rush on the pigs' trotters. At such times the merchant class stands alone, ordering the tumult of desire into the ledgerly rhythm of exchange with a composure as implacable as a cottage loaf. Tongue.

(*During the speech* WEINBERL *has folded his letter and put it in an envelope.* CHRISTOPHER *sticks out his tongue and* WEINBERL *dabs a postage stamp on the tongue and slaps it on the envelope. He seals the envelope with satisfaction.*)

CHRISTOPHER: How is your romance, Herr Weinberl?

WEINBERL: As well as can be expected of a relationship based on pseudonymous correspondence between two post office boxes. One has to proceed cautiously with lonely hearts advertisements. There is a great deal of self-delusion among these women—although I must admit I am becoming very taken with the one who signs herself Elegant And Under Forty. I am thinking of coming out from behind my own nom de plume of Scaramouche. The trouble is, I rather think I have given her the impression that I am more or less the owner of this place, not to mention others like it ...

CHRISTOPHER: At least you're not a dogsbody like me.

WEINBERL: Dogsbody? You're an apprentice. You've had a valuable training during your five years under me.

CHRISTOPHER: You see things differently from the dizzy heights of chief sales assistant.

WEINBERL: Christopher, Christopher, have a pretzel ... The dignity of labour embraces servant and master, for every master is a servant too, answerable to the voice of a higher authority.

ZANGLER: (*Outside*) Weinberl!

(*Without seeming to hurry* WEINBERL *instantly puts things to order.*)

WEINBERL: I thought you said he'd gone.

CHRISTOPHER: He must have changed his mind.

(ZANGLER *enters from the house.*)

ZANGLER: Ah, there you are. Is it time to open the shop?

WEINBERL: Not quite, Chief. I was just getting everything straight.

ZANGLER: What about this pretzel?

WEINBERL: The pretzel defeated me completely. (*To* CHRISTOPHER.) Put it back. Are you going to the parade, Herr Zangler?

ZANGLER: No, I'm going beagling. What do you think?

WEINBERL: I think you're making fun of me, Chief.

ZANGLER: How does it look?

WEINBERL: (*Tactfully*) Snug.

ZANGLER: Do you think it should be let out?

WEINBERL: Not till after dark.

ZANGLER: What?

WEINBERL: No.

ZANGLER: Are you sure?

WEINBERL: I like it, Chief.

CHRISTOPHER: I like it.

ZANGLER: I can't deny it's smart. Did you notice the spurs?

(*The spurs announce themselves every time* ZANGLER *moves.*)

WEINBERL: The spurs? Oh yes . . .

CHRISTOPHER: I noticed them.

ZANGLER: I'm rather pleased with the effect. I feel like the cake of the week.

WEINBERL: That's very well put, Chief.

ZANGLER: I don't mean the cake of the week—

WEINBERL: Not the cake of the week—the Sheikh of Kuwait—

ZANGLER: No—

CHRISTOPHER: The clerk of the works—

ZANGLER: No!

WEINBERL: The cock of the walk?

ZANGLER: That's the boy. I feel like the cock of the walk.

WEINBERL: You'll be the pride of the Sporting and Benevolent Musical Fusiliers of the Grocers' Company, and what wonderful work they do for the widows and orphans.

ZANGLER: I was just setting off when I suddenly had doubts.

WEINBERL: I assure you, without people like the grocers there'd be no widows and orphans at all.

25

ZANGLER: No, I mean I had doubts about leaving.

WEINBERL: I don't understand you, Chief.

ZANGLER: My niece and ward is preying on my mind. There's something not quite right there.

CHRISTOPHER: My niece and ward *are* preying on my mind—?

ZANGLER: (*Ignoring him*) Something not quite the ticket. Sonders is a dyed-in-the-wool Don Juan. He's turned Marie's head and for all I know she's already lost it.

WEINBERL: Well, she didn't lose it in shop-hours.

ZANGLER: I'm going to frustrate him.

WEINBERL: Frustration is too good for him, Chief.

ZANGLER: I'm sending Marie away for a few days. You'll have to manage the while the till . . . No—

WEINBERL: To while the time . . .

ZANGLER: No!

WEINBERL: The till the while?

ZANGLER: That's the boy. You'll have to manage the till the while, and do the books at the close of business. I suppose you're prepared to do that?

WEINBERL: Very well prepared if I may say so, Herr Zangler.

ZANGLER: There will be other changes. Prepare yourself for a surprise. I have always prided myself on being a good master who has made every reasonable provision for his staff.

WEINBERL: You have, Chief.

ZANGLER: Well, what would you say to having a mistress?

CHRISTOPHER: One each or sharing?

WEINBERL: Congratulations, Chief! We wish you and your bride every happiness.

ZANGLER: Thank you, thank you.

WEINBERL: May one ask who is the fortunate young lady?

ZANGLER: Actually she's a widow, in business like me. Well not actually like me, far from it, it's a haute couture house catering exclusively to the beau monde with three girls working upstairs. What do you say to that?

WEINBERL: Well, there's not a lot you can say, Chief.

ZANGLER: What the devil is the matter with everybody! That's another thing that was worrying me—leaving the place in charge of you two. I need someone with a proper sense of

26

responsibility, not a log-rolling counter-clerk and a cack-handed apprentice.

WEINBERL: I'm mortified.

CHRISTOPHER: I'm articled.

WEINBERL: Who have you got in mind, Chief?

ZANGLER: Well, you two of course!

WEINBERL: I mean to put in charge with a sense of responsibility?

ZANGLER: What would you do in my shoes?

WEINBERL: Jingle.

ZANGLER: What?

WEINBERL: Jingle make any difference just for one afternoon, Chief?

ZANGLER: It may be longer. The duration of my absence will depend on how things go at a certain engagement I have this evening. Meanwhile desperate situations call for desperate measures. Master Christopher! Approach!

CHRISTOPHER: He called me Master. Is it the sack?

ZANGLER: I've been paying for your clothes all these years, as you know.

CHRISTOPHER: No, I thought you bought them outright when you took me on.

WEINBERL: Shut up.

ZANGLER: By rights you owe me another six months' apprenticeship, but to celebrate my nuptials I have decided to forgo those months. I am appointing you chief sales assistant.

WEINBERL: Such an honour is granted to such a few. Show your gratitude, then. He's stunned, Chief.

CHRISTOPHER: Chief sales assistant! Oh, Herr Zangler, your bountifulness!

ZANGLER: You may call me Chief. Stop snivelling—where's your—

CHRISTOPHER: Thank you, Chief!

ZANGLER: Thank-you-Chief—no—

WEINBERL (*Worried*) Hang on, Chief—

ZANGLER: Hang-on-Chief—no!—

CHRISTOPHER: Will I have my ceremony, Chief? I've got to have my—

ZANGLER: What?

CHRISTOPHER: Initiation, Chief!

ZANGLER: Bless you. And we must have the ceremony. Raise
your right trouser and repeat after me . . . I swear.

CHRISTOPHER: I swear . . .

ZANGLER: Weinberl, do you remember how it goes?

WEINBERL: To strive and to abide.

CHRISTOPHER: To strive and to abide.

WEINBERL: No—I swear by the sacred apron of the Grand
Victualler—no—it's been a long time . . .

CHRISTOPHER: (*Rapidly*) I swear by the sacred apron of the
Imperial Grand Grocer and by the grocery chain of his
office, to strive for his victualler in freehold, to abide by his
argument which flows from his premises, to honour his
custom, keep up his stock, give credit to few, be credit to
all, and not be found wanting when weighed in the scales,
so help me God!

ZANGLER: You may jump the counter.

(CHRISTOPHER *jumps*.)

That's that. I will inform you of changes in your duties
should any occur to me—except of course that you have to
buy your own clothes.

CHRISTOPHER: Thank you, Chief!

ZANGLER: And remember, always give people their change
between finger and thumb. Nothing lets down the tone of a
place so much as change from the fist.

CHRISTOPHER: Right, Chief.

WEINBERL: Excuse me, Chief. Am I your chief sales assistant or
am I not?

ZANGLER: You are not. I have decided to make you my partner.
To take effect from the day of my marriage.

WEINBERL: (*Stunned*) Me? Your partner?

ZANGLER: Yes. As a married man who has come into possession
of a couture establishment I will be spending more time
away from here. It's only right that you should have an
interest in the prosperity of the business, and probably
cheaper.

WEINBERL: Partner . . .

ZANGLER: Yes, yes, as soon as my bride has consummated my
expansion into her turnover you will be my partner. If you

28

strive and abide you may find yourself in my old uniform. Now—what shall I do? Shall I go or what?

WEINBERL: What . . .?

ZANGLER: No, I'll go.

CHRISTOPHER: Good luck, Chief!

ZANGLER: I'm going to join the parade and call on my fiancée— It's her birthday. I'm hoping to have a little sextet outside her hat shop before I take her to dinner.

CHRISTOPHER: Outside? In the street?

ZANGLER: Yes. I can't help it. I'm a fool to myself when I'm in love. If I'm not back by morning you'll know where I'll be.

CHRISTOPHER: In jail?

ZANGLER: In the milliner's arms.

CHRISTOPHER: Have one for me, Chief!

ZANGLER: What?—No. I will go and plait my truss—no—

CHRISTOPHER: Plight your—

ZANGLER: That's the boy!

(ZANGLER *goes*.)

WEINBERL: (*In a daze*) Partner . . . partner . . . I'm a partner. One moment a put-upon counter-clerk, the next a pillar of the continental trading community.

CHRISTOPHER: Chief sales assistant . . . I've always been at the bottom of the ladder and now . . . (*A thought strikes him*.) Who's going to be under me, then?

WEINBERL: Book-keeper—that was the Himalaya of my aspirations, but from the vantage point of partnership I look tolerantly down upon the book-keeper's place as if from a throne of clouds.

CHRISTOPHER: He's a partner and I'm the entire staff. I'll have two masters instead of one, three counting the widow, and the weight of my authority will be felt by the housekeeper's cat.

WEINBERL: And yet—strangely enough—now, now of all times, when fortune has smiled upon me like a lunatic upon a worm in an apple, I feel a sense of . . . (*Pause*) grief.

CHRISTOPHER: That cat is going to wish it had never been born.

WEINBERL: What is happening to me? I feel a loosening of obscure restraints . . . Desires stir in my breast like shifting crates on a badly loaded barrow.

CHRISTOPHER: (*Breaks out*) Oh, Mother, what is the wherefore of it all?!—Whither the striving and how the abiding for a poor boy in the grocery trade? I'm glad she's dead and doesn't see me chained to this counter like a dog to a kennel, knowing nothing of the world except what happens to get wrapped around the next pound of groceries. Seeing the sunrise only from an attic window, and the sunset reflected in a row of spice jars, agog at travellers' tales of paved streets! Oh, Mr Weinberl, I have come into my kingdom and I see that it is the locked room from which you celebrate your escape! And if I have to wait until I am as old as you, *that's longer than I've been alive!*

WEINBERL: (*Soberly*) Beyond the door is another room. The servant is the slave of his master and the master is the slave of his business.

CHRISTOPHER: (*Regarding* ZANGLER's *old uniform left in the room*) Try it on.

WEINBERL: What?

CHRISTOPHER: Try it on.

WEINBERL: No—

CHRISTOPHER: Go on!

WEINBERL: Gertrud might come in—I mustn't!

CHRISTOPHER: All right.

WEINBERL: I daren't!

CHRISTOPHER: All right.

WEINBERL: Dare I? (*He starts to don the uniform.*) If only I could look back on a day when I was fancy free, a real razzle of a day packed with adventure and high jinks, a day to remember when I am a grand-grocer jingling through Vienna in my boots and spurs and the livery of the Grocers' Company or passing the grog and spinning the yarn with the merchant princes of the retail trade, when I could say, 'Oh, I was a gay dog in my day, a real rapscallion —why, I remember once . . .' but I have nothing to remember.

(*Desperately*) I've got to acquire a past before it's too late!

CHRISTOPHER: Can I come with you, Mr Weinberl?

WEINBERL: Come with me where?

CHRISTOPHER: I want it now!

WEINBERL: Now?

CHRISTOPHER: This very minute!

WEINBERL: (*Appalled*) What? Lock up the shop?

CHRISTOPHER: It's already locked.

WEINBERL: While he's at the parade . . .?

CHRISTOPHER: And dinner in town. It's only us two. Marie is
  confined to quarters. He'll never know.

WEINBERL: Wait . . . (*He paces about feverishly and then
  embraces* CHRISTOPHER.) What about the books?

CHRISTOPHER: We'll cook the books!

WEINBERL: Yes!—what about the cook?

CHRISTOPHER: We'll fix the cook. We'll tell her he told us to tell
  her he told us he doesn't want to open the shop.

WEINBERL: What happens when she tells him we told her he told
  us to tell her he told us—

CHRISTOPHER: The cook . . .

GERTRUD: (*Offstage*) Isn't it time you opened the shop—it's gone
  two o'clock.

WEINBERL: She'll do for us . . . Get me out of this!
  (CHRISTOPHER *pulls the uniform tunic over* WEINBERL's *head.*
  GERTRUD *appears.*)

GERTRUD: So you're still in two minds, Herr Zangler?

CHRISTOPHER: He is, and he's half out of both of them.
  (*To* WEINBERL *loudly*) It's Gertrud, Herr Zangler . . . Get
  it?
  (*All* WEINBERL's *lines are muffled and unintelligible and
  furious.* WEINBERL *speaks.*)

WEINBERL: Got it!

GERTRUD: Twenty-three Carlstrasse, Miss Blumenblatt's.
  (*This is the wrong answer and* WEINBERL *speaks even more
  furiously.*)

CHRISTOPHER: Master says find Mr Weinberl and tell him not to
  open the shop this afternoon.

GERTRUD: Don't open the shop. Tell Mr Weinberl.
  (WEINBERL *again.*)

CHRISTOPHER: Strict orders, he says, and now he would be
  obliged if you would be so kind as to leave him.

GERTRUD: That doesn't sound like him.
  (WEINBERL *dances about and roars.* CHRISTOPHER *goes as*

though to help him into the tunic. GERTRUD *speaks as she leaves.)* ·

That does.

CHRISTOPHER: *(Pulling the tunic over* WEINBERL's *head)* She's gone.

WEINBERL: And now, best foot forward.

CHRISTOPHER: I'll get my worsted stocking.

WEINBERL: Is that necessary?

CHRISTOPHER: It's got my savings in it.

WEINBERL: I'll get mine and we'll be off.

(Door slam and jingle of spurs.)

ZANGLER: *(Offstage)* Gertrud!

WEINBERL: God in heaven he's back again!

*(*CHRISTOPHER *picks up* WEINBERL's *discarded clothes and runs off towards the shop. Spurs however still approach.)*

I can't let him see me like this!

(Before WEINBERL *can follow* CHRISTOPHER, GERTRUD *enters from the kitchen and* WEINBERL *dives behind the furniture.* ZANGLER *enters at the same time.)*

ZANGLER: *(Shouts)* Marie! Damn and blast it, that swinehound Sonders is nowhere to be seen in the village, and he didn't leave on the coach and Marie's window is open! God in Himalayas!—If I keep having to come back I'll miss the parade. I told you not to let Marie out of your sight.

GERTRUD: You told me to find Weinberl and tell him—

ZANGLER: Don't tell me what I told you—search her room. If she's got out of her Scottish get-up, ten to one he's up there trying it on. I'll keep watch in the garden if I can find a place to hide.

GERTRUD: Stand in the herbaceous border.

(They leave in different directions. WEINBERL *comes out from behind the furniture and runs into the shop, looking for his clothes.)*

Zangler's shop

WEINBERL *enters, calling for* CHRISTOPHER. *But he has only just entered when the trap door in the floor starts coming up and he dives into a cupboard, or perhaps under the counter.* SONDERS *and* MARIE, *dressed in a voluminous, tartan, hooded cape, emerge from the cellar.*

SONDERS: It's all right—it's deserted—courage mon amour—

MARIE: Oh, August—we mustn't—it's not proper.

SONDERS: Now's our chance—we can escape by the shop door while they're searching round the back.

MARIE: Oh, but it's not proper.

SONDERS: Don't you love me?

MARIE: You know I love you but I don't want to run away—

SONDERS: Elopement isn't running away, it's running towards.

MARIE: It's not proper.

SONDERS: Is it proper for your guardian to behave as if he owns you?

MARIE: Yes. That's why they call it property. I think. Oh, August, you're a terrible man, kiss me again. You made me feel all funny down there.

(He embraces her, more inside her cape than out.)

SONDERS: Oh, Marie!

MARIE: I mean in the cellar—Oh, somebody's coming!

SONDERS: Hide in here!

MARIE: No, it isn't prop—!

(He dives into WEINBERL'S *cupboard, pulling her after him.* CHRISTOPHER *enters from a second door with* WEINBERL'S *clothes, calling for him and running out of the shop. The cupboard door bursts open.* MARIE *comes out,* SONDERS *comes out and* WEINBERL'S *legs come out.* WEINBERL *is lying on his front.)*

SONDERS: Someone has been eavesdropping on us—

MARIE: I thought it was a squash in there.

*(*SONDERS *drags* WEINBERL *out by his heels, or spurs. He and* MARIE *are aghast to find that* ZANGLER *seems to be lying on the floor with his face still in the cupboard.* SONDERS *and* MARIE *kneel down and bow their heads as* WEINBERL *gets unsteadily to his feet.* WEINBERL *gazes down on to the crowns of their heads.)*

MARIE: Oh, my uncle!

SONDERS: Oh, my God—Herr Zangler!

MARIE: Don't be angry, dear Uncle, I meant no harm.

SONDERS: She's blameless, sir, intact I swear, I mean in fact I

33

swear she did it against her will.

MARIE: I *didn't* do it!

SONDERS: No she didn't—I haven't—Oh, sir, it was love that drove us to deceive you!

(*They are kissing* WEINBERL's *hands.*)

MARIE: Won't you speak to me, Uncle? Your harshest words are easier to bear than the silence of your anger.

(WEINBERL, *deeply embarrassed, disengages his hands and pats the two heads.*)

SONDERS: What do you . . .?

MARIE: Do you mean . . .?

(*They try to raise their heads but* WEINBERL *firmly keeps their heads down and presses them together.*)

SONDERS: He's blessing our union.

(WEINBERL *guides their faces into a lingering kiss during which he is able to retire, silently, from the room.*)

SONDERS: Marie!

MARIE: Oh, August!

Oh, Uncle, you've made me so . . . Where has he gone?

SONDERS: What a surprising man he is! Beneath his rough manners he is the very soul of tact.

MARIE: (*Getting up*) I always knew he was shy underneath.

SONDERS: Let me kiss you again.

MARIE: You can kiss me properly now!

(*They go into another lingering kiss, during which* ZANGLER *enters. He has a silent apoplexy. At length* SONDERS *notices him.*)

SONDERS: (*Suavely*) Ah, there you are, my dear sir, we were wondering where you'd got to.

ZANGLER: (*Strangled*) Sonders! (*A couple of buttons fly off his uniform.*)

MARIE: Oh, you must call him August now—you're going to be such friends—isn't he handsome?

ZANGLER: I'll kill him.

MARIE: Uncle, but you just—

ZANGLER: Slut!

SONDERS: My dear sir, what can have happened?

ZANGLER: You blackguard! You barefaced dastardly—

SONDERS: He's mad.

34

(GERTRUD *enters.*)

GERTRUD: (*Placidly*) Oh, you've found them.

MARIE: Oh, Uncle, you're not yourself . . .

ZANGLER: I'll make you eat your words, you ungrateful little Messalina!

GERTRUD: Make you eat your semolina you ungrateful little—

ZANGLER: (*Screams*) Shut up!

MARIE: Oh . . . (*She runs weeping from the room.*)

SONDERS: Marie!

GERTRUD: She's upset, I can tell.

(GERTRUD *exits, following Marie.*)

SONDERS: This is absurd—I'll come back when you're feeling calmer.

(ZANGLER *chases* SONDERS *out.*)

ZANGLER: You dare to show your nose in here again and I'll cut off your coquette to spite your face! And furthermore I'll disinherit her!

(*This takes* ZANGLER *out of the room.* WEINBERL, *in his own clothes, and* CHRISTOPHER *reappear. They are gleeful.*)

WEINBERL: Christopher . . . Did you hear that?

CHRISTOPHER: (*Looking down the street*) He's still running. I don't think he'll ever come back.

WEINBERL: Oh my! I feel like a real rapscallion. We're on the razzle at last! (*They embrace.*)

(*Enter* WEINBERL *riding horse,* CHRISTOPHER *leading them.*)

WEINBERL: We've done it! We're on the razzle! We're going to get a past at last!

CHRISTOPHER: (*Disappointed*) Is this what a razzle is like, Mr Weinberl?

WEINBERL: No—not yet—wait till we really get into our stride. (*To horse*) Come on Lightning . . .

CHRISTOPHER: How far is Vienna, Mr Weinberl?

WEINBERL: It's a long way, Christopher.

CHRISTOPHER: How large is Vienna, Mr Weinberl?

WEINBERL: It is very large, Christopher . . . Whoa, Lightning . . .

(WEINBERL *gets off, and* CHRISTOPHER *gets on the horse.*)

Giddy up, Lightning.

CHRISTOPHER: Will there be women, Mr Weinberl?

WEINBERL: Beautiful women, Christopher.

CHRISTOPHER: How old are the women in Vienna, Mr Weinberl?

WEINBERL: Twenty-two, Christopher.

CHRISTOPHER: How does one meet them, Mr Weinberl?

WEINBERL: They promenade in packs, with parasols, and gloves up to here. They consort with cosmopolitan men-of-the-world in the fashionable cafés.

CHRISTOPHER: I have read that they are often kept, Mr Weinberl.

WEINBERL: Kept for what, Christopher?

CHRISTOPHER: That's what always puzzled *me*.

WEINBERL: Whoa, Lightning. Vienna, Christopher, is the place to find out . . . Look!

(*They are looking out over Vienna.*)

CHRISTOPHER: (*Impressed*) It's just like you said . . .

WEINBERL: (*Enchanted*) It is, isn't it?

Arriving in Vienna . . . gaiety and music . . . CHRISTOPHER *takes it all in wide-eyed. The dialogue is part of the set change.*

CHRISTOPHER: Is the city always like this, Mr Weinberl? All this gay panoply . . .

WEINBERL: (*Slightly puzzled*) Well . . . more or less . . .

CHRISTOPHER: (*Enthusiastically*) Bands playing—streets full of colourful costumes—it's like a great parade . . .

WEINBERL: (*Thoughtfully*) Yes . . .

CHRISTOPHER: What would old Zangler think if he saw us now?

WEINBERL: Oh yes . . .!

(*The penny drops.*)

Parade?!

CHRISTOPHER: Parade!

(*The parade is going right by them.*)

WEINBERL: My God, suppose Zangler happens to—There he is!—get down . . .

(WEINBERL *and* CHRISTOPHER *obviously see* ZANGLER *approaching. The parade music suddenly incorporates the massed spurs of the Grocers' Company.* CHRISTOPHER *dismounts and he and* WEINBERL *exit under cover of Lightning.*)

Annagasse exterior—Madame Knorr's Fashion House
Distant parade. CHRISTOPHER *and* WEINBERL *enter running. They come to a breathless halt outside the windows which flank the entrance door of the fashion house. Windows above.*

CHRISTOPHER: Well, we *nearly* had an adventure.

WEINBERL: Yes that *would* have been our final fling if Zangler had caught sight of us.

CHRISTOPHER: On the other hand we don't want to end up flingless . . .

WEINBERL: Dishonoured and unflung . . .

CHRISTOPHER: You're not downhearted, are you?

WEINBERL: I don't know. I've been getting a sharp stabbing pain just here.

CHRISTOPHER: You've got the stitch.

WEINBERL: I don't think so. It only happens when I see an open grocer's shop. It'll be just my luck if I've got Weinberl's Disease.

CHRISTOPHER: It would certainly be a coincidence. Still, it sounds like the sort of thing people come to Vienna for from all over the world, so to get it while you're here on a rare visit smacks of outrageous good fortune. I'm trying to make you look on the bright side.

WEINBERL: Christopher.

CHRISTOPHER: Yes, Mr Weinberl?

WEINBERL: Embrace me. What happened to Lightning?

CHRISTOPHER: She always turns up.

WEINBERL: What will we do if she's gone?

CHRISTOPHER: We'll bolt the stable door.

WEINBERL: And keep mum.

CHRISTOPHER: If only she could see me now. . . . Well, where's the razzle?

WEINBERL: There's plenty of time. There's probably an adventure laying in wait for us at this very spot.
(PHILIPPINE *seen moving about inside, putting the lights on. The light illuminates, for the first time, the words 'Knorr's Fashion House'.*)

WEINBERL: For all we know we have made an appointment with destiny.

CHRISTOPHER: Nothing is going to happen to us in a pokey little cul-de-sac like this.

WEINBERL: The parade must be over. Let's go.

CHRISTOPHER: We might run into the boss.

WEINBERL: No, no—he's got the whole of Vienna to choose from, there's absolutely no reason why . . .
(*Distant footfalls and jingle of spurs approach. The little street echos with the sound.*)

WEINBERL: It's Nemesis!

CHRISTOPHER: Well, he's got Zangler with him!
(*They run in opposite directions, then change their minds, then rush through the doorway into the shop. Their faces appear in the windows, one in each, watching the street cautiously as* ZANGLER *comes into view.* To their consternation* ZANGLER *walks straight to the shop. The faces disappear. As* ZANGLER *turns the door handle, two voluminously swathed tartan mannequins leap into the windows, one in each. At the same moment* MELCHIOR *runs in from the side while* ZANGLER *is in the doorway.*)

MELCHIOR: Sir!—Oh what luck! The Classinova person—the whosit incarnate—the Don Juan is at the Imperial Gardens Café with a nice young lady like a ladylike young niece!

ZANGLER: (*Emerging confused*) Eh, what? What? Who's this?

MELCHIOR: Herr Zangler!

ZANGLER: Your servant, sir—no, by God it's mine. What are you doing here?

MELCHIOR: I came to find you, your eminence.

ZANGLER: I told you to go straight to the restaurant.

MELCHIOR: I did but the Cassata incarnate has arrived and the tart!

ZANGLER: But that's just desserts. What about my dinner?

MELCHIOR: The dinner is all arranged, but I'm on the trail of the Casserola and you must come immediately before it gets cold.

ZANGLER: Tell them to put it in the oven. You seem to lack a sense of proportion. I am about to present myself to my fiancée in no uncertain terms, and I'm damned if I'm

---

* In the original production Zangler was accompanied by the 'little sextet' which serenaded the windows until summarily dismissed by Zangler after Melchior's arrival.

going to be harried and put off my stroke by the ridiculous self-importance of a jumped-up pastry-cook. Honestly, these fashionable eating houses, they think they're doing you a favour by taking your money. I told you to wait for me.

MELCHIOR: I was waiting for you, sir, and who should arrive by horsecab but the very same seducer I saw leave your home.

ZANGLER: There you are, you see!—I should have remained true to the Black and White Chop House.

MELCHIOR: He had a young woman with him.

ZANGLER: Of course he did—it must be three or four hours since he found himself with a vacancy.

MELCHIOR: She was in a Scottish get-up.

ZANGLER: Vienna has been overrun with Scottish get-ups, kilts, tam-o'-shanters, Royal Stuart pencil cases and highland flingery of every stripe since the town lost its head over the Verdi *Macbeth*. In my opinion it's a disgrace. Even the chocolate cake . . . Sachertartan! No, no, a Scottish get-up means nothing—there's even two in the window here . . . (WEINBERL *and* CHRISTOPHER *hastily resume rigidity. They mustn't have a proper view of* MELCHIOR, *by the way*.) Damn it, are you deliberately trying to prick my bubble while I stand knocking at my fiancée's main entrance?

MELCHIOR: He called her Marie.

ZANGLER: A very common name. I told Gertrud to put Marie into a locked cab and give the coachman an extra fiver if he delivered her personally into the hands of my sister-in-law, Miss Blumenblatt. What could be surer than that?

MELCHIOR: A fiver? Yes, I would say that we must be talking of two different Maries.

ZANGLER: Exactly. And what yours does is no concern of mine.

MELCHIOR: I don't think she'll do much. I had a listen and all she said was 'It's not proper.'

ZANGLER: It's them!

MELCHIOR: No, no, a tart and ward of an entirely different clan.

ZANGLER: It's them!! Quick, fetch me a half-witted cab you hansom fool!

MELCHIOR: We're off!

ZANGLER: (*Leaving*) What a situation!

MELCHIOR: (*Following him*) Classic!

39

Madame Knorr's Fashion House

WEINBERL *and* CHRISTOPHER *come out of the windows into the shop.*
CHRISTOPHER *disrobes.* WEINBERL *is late and* PHILIPPINE *enters.*
WEINBERL *starts sashaying round the shop in his tartan cloak, for*
CHRISTOPHER's *benefit.*

WEINBERL: What do you think?

CHRISTOPHER: It has a certain Scottish audacity.

WEINBERL: Ah, there you are at last. Am I addressing the
arbiter of this fashion house?

PHILIPPINE: I'm sure I don't know, sir. I will fetch Madame at
once. But excuse me, sir, that is a lady's cape.

WEINBERL: I know. I was trying it on for a lady of my size and
acquaintance.

PHILIPPINE: That cape is reserved. It has a ticket on it.

WEINBERL: Yes. I know. (*Reads the ticket.*) Frau Fischer. I have
come to collect it and pay for it.

CHRISTOPHER: Not exactly to pay for it.

WEINBERL: No, not exactly to pay for it, but to confirm payment.
(CHRISTOPHER *has been looking out cautiously through the*
windows.)

CHRISTOPHER: I think it is all clear now, Herr Fischer.

WEINBERL: Is that clear?

PHILIPPINE: I'm not sure. I'd better go and fetch Madame.

WEINBERL: Excellent idea.

CHRISTOPHER: Meanwhile we'll be off.

WEINBERL: -ally grateful if you would take care of this. (*He*
hands her the cape grandly.)

PHILIPPINE: Yes, sir. Did you say Herr Fischer?

WEINBERL: Certainly. Would I pay—

CHRISTOPHER: Confirm payment.

WEINBERL: Confirm payment for somebody else's wife? (*To*
CHRISTOPHER.) Why don't you see if our friend is anywhere
in sight?

CHRISTOPHER: Good idea. I'll be back in a moment.

WEINBERL: Is anything the matter?

PHILIPPINE: Frau Fischer has been a widow for three years.

WEINBERL: She thinks she has, yes.

PHILIPPINE: She thinks she has? What about the funeral?

WEINBERL: It was the funeral that put the idea into her head.

40

That she'd always be a widow. However, three days ago she did me the honour of becoming my wife.

(*To* CHRISTOPHER *who has paused in admiration on his way out*) You will come back, won't you?

(CHRISTOPHER *goes*.)

PHILIPPINE: I'll fetch Madame immediately. She's upstairs in the workroom.

WEINBERL: Tell her there's no hurry—she's probably busy hemming and hawing.

(PHILIPPINE *goes but instantly returns*.)

PHILIPPINE: But, Herr Fischer, why didn't Frau Fischer change her name to yours instead of you changing your name to hers?

WEINBERL: She did. I didn't. My name, as it happens, is also Fischer. That's how we met. We were placed in alphabetical order in a fire drill at the riding academy.

PHILIPPINE: Oh, I see.

(PHILIPPINE *goes*. WEINBERL *looks cautiously into the street. While he is so engaged*, MRS FISCHER *enters the shop.* WEINBERL *bows to her and continues to look out of the window for* CHRISTOPHER'S *return. After a few moments* MADAME KNORR *enters, gushing*.)

MME KNORR: There they are!—They're both here! And what a couple of naughty children you are!—Oh, my dear friend, why didn't you tell me?

MRS FISCHER: Are you feeling all right, my dear?

MME KNORR: No, I am not feeling all right. I am feeling distinctly put out. Fancy being married for three whole days without saying a word to your oldest friend and leaving your husband to break the news.

(MRS FISCHER *follows* MADAME KNORR'S *gaze towards* WEINBERL.)

However, I forgive you . . . (*She walks round* WEINBERL.) And now that I see your husband I can quite understand why you kept him hidden away.

MRS FISCHER: My husband? (*She examines* WEINBERL *with interest*.) And he announced our marriage himself did he?

(WEINBERL *flinches from her gaze, particularly when she gets out her lorgnettes to scrutinize him all the better*. MADAME

KNORR *keeps gushing.*)

MME KNORR: And none too soon. It is such an honour to meet you. I think it is so romantic—you must have swept her off her feet. Tell me, how long have you known each other?

MRS FISCHER: Not long at all.

WEINBERL: No, not long.

MME KNORR: You must have been married with your head in a whirl!

MRS FISCHER: You couldn't say I went into it with my eyes open.

MME KNORR: Of course you did, and I am sure you have not been disappointed.

MRS FISCHER: Surprised more than disappointed. My husband has a very individual way of dealing with the banalities of ordinary time—I expect we'll be engaged next week and exchange cards the week after.

MME KNORR: Isn't she priceless?

WEINBERL: I expect you think I'm rather presumptuous.

MRS FISCHER: No, I wouldn't say you were presumptuous. Presumption one has encountered before.

WEINBERL: Well, a little forward.

MRS FISCHER: A little forward? You will meet yourself coming back.

MME KNORR: But why so sudden and secret?

MRS FISCHER: There was a reason. My dear husband will tell you.

MME KNORR: Oh do tell.

WEINBERL: My dear wife can tell you just as well as I.

MRS FISCHER: But I would like *you* to tell her.

WEINBERL: And I would like *you* to tell her—after all she's your friend.

MME KNORR: Oh dear, not quarrelling already!

MRS FISCHER: It was a whim of my dear husband's.

WEINBERL: And at the same time a whim of my dear wife's.

MME KNORR: But it is extraordinary.

WEINBERL: There is nothing extraordinary about it. When two attractive people . . .

MME KNORR: A marriage of true minds.

MRS FISCHER: Entirely.

WEINBERL: Yes, indeed. Well, I must be going.

MRS FISCHER: Going? What do you mean?

42

WEINBERL: I have some business to attend to.

MRS FISCHER: Aren't you going to see me try on my new Scottish cape? After all it wouldn't be fair if you didn't like it.

WEINBERL: Why?

MRS FISCHER: (*To* MADAME KNORR, *joshingly*) Why?!—isn't he the soul of generosity? If I like something, that's enough for him.

WEINBERL: Actually, I think this tartan fad has had its fling, you know.

MRS FISCHER: Had its fling!—such a sense of humour. We'll take it.

MME KNORR: (*To* WEINBERL) Will it be cash or account?

WEINBERL: Account, I think. Well, if that's all you wanted . . . Delighted to have met you at last—my wife has told me so much about you.

MRS FISCHER: Don't be so impatient, my dear—I've had such a wonderful idea.

WEINBERL: One needs a lot of patience in a marriage, I find.

MRS FISCHER: I hope I've never given you cause for complaint.

WEINBERL: Oh no.

MRS FISCHER: Have I ever contradicted you on matters large or small?

WEINBERL: No never—much appreciated.

MRS FISCHER: Don't I do my best to enter into your ideas against all reason?

WEINBERL: You do, you do. And since you make a point of doing so I am sure you won't mind if I now leave you with your friend and your Scottish cape and go about my business.

MRS FISCHER: I would mind very much. Out of courtesy to Madame Knorr I cannot let you forget that your only business today is to take us out to a celebration supper.

MME KNORR: A celebration supper! Isn't fate extraordinary! I was hoping my fiancée would pin me down at the Black and White Chop House tonight, but, not for the first time, he preferred to stand me up.

WEINBERL: Did he?

MME KNORR: He did.*

* The next seven speeches apply only if ZANGLER's sextet has put in its appearance in the street scene.

43

I thought I would be getting a little gold band.

WEINBERL: And you didn't?

MME KNORR: I did not. It turned out to be a little brass band.

WEINBERL: Did it?

MME KNORR: It did.

WEINBERL: Did your finger turn green?

MME KNORR: *I* turned green. But now the evening promises to turn out just as memorable.

MRS FISCHER: So you will oblige us, won't you?

WEINBERL: I would adore to but alas—

MRS FISCHER: Very well!—Eugenia, my dear, I'm afraid I have to tell you—that this man—

WEINBERL: Why don't we all walk around to the Black and White Chop House and raise a foaming tankard to our happiness. And after that I really must dash.

MRS FISCHER: The Black and White Chop House? I'm sure it will cause no surprise to anyone here that you would prefer to treat us to somewhere a little better than that. I can change into my new Scottish ensemble. We'll need a cab.

MME KNORR: That's a wonderful idea! I do think your wife deserves a kiss for that.

WEINBERL: Do you think so?

MME KNORR: Oh, I do!

WEINBERL: Well, I'm not going to deny anyone their due. Permit me.

(WEINBERL *kisses* MRS FISCHER, *to her embarrassment.*)

MME KNORR: Do you call that a kiss? You don't have to stand on ceremony in front of me.

WEINBERL: Oh very well. (*He gives her a lingering kiss on the mouth.*) And in case my bride has any more good ideas I'll give her one on account.

(*He kisses her again.* CHRISTOPHER *enters the shop.*)

CHRISTOPHER: All clear.

WEINBERL: Ah, there you are. I don't think you've met my wife. This is my cousin from the country. I'm the kissing cousin, he's the country cousin. My wife—my wife's friend, Madame Knorr—my cousin—the four of us are going to have supper together at . . . (*He looks enquiringly at* MRS FISCHER.)

MRS FISCHER: The Imperial Gardens Café.

WEINBERL: The Imperial Gardens Café. Where else? Go and fetch a cab . . .

(*He ushers* CHRISTOPHER *out.*)

He'll be back in a few moments.

MRS FISCHER: We'll keep the cab and go on somewhere else.

WEINBERL: Another good idea!

(*He takes her into a passionate embrace.* CHRISTOPHER *comes out of his daze. He gives a cry of delight, throws his hat in the air and runs off down the street.*)

ACT TWO

The Imperial Gardens Café

This is a conservatory ante-room. The main restaurant is off stage. Large window in back wall, through which are visible some of the garden, terrace, etc., and a partial view of a hansom cab, possibly with horse attached. There is a door into this garden. There are in-and-out swing doors to the kitchen. Stairs from the main area lead up to a gallery at the back, from which a window looks out over the garden where the cab is.

The place is fashionable, even pretentious; the clientele likewise. At curtain-up we find a traffic of customers, waiters, etc. passing through while music plays. The women's dresses suggest that the town has gone mad for tartan. There is also a disconcerting Scottish influence in the Vienna waltzes; bagpipes have been imported.

There are two dining tables, some chairs, a coatstand. There is a folding screen of Chinese design.

The fashionable scene disperses and the music comes to an end.

After a pause the disembodied voices of ZANGLER *and* MELCHIOR, *who are hidden on the stage, are heard.*

ZANGLER: Melchior.

MELCHIOR: Herr Zangler.

ZANGLER: What's happened to the music?

MELCHIOR: Yes, I know. It's partly the influence of German Pessimism, partly the decadence of an Empire that has outlived its purpose, and partly Scottish fortnight. I don't hold with it myself. Give me the evergreens every time, that's what I say, those golden oldies of yesteryear, the Blue Danube, and that other one—

ZANGLER: Melchior.

MELCHIOR: Yes, Herr Zangler.

46

ZANGLER: Shut up or I'll kill you.

MELCHIOR: Very good, Herr Zangler.

(A jingle of spurs announces ZANGLER's appearance. He is wittily revealed on the stage. MELCHIOR remains invisible. ZANGLER evidently doesn't know where MELCHIOR is hiding.)

ZANGLER: *(Looking round)* Melchior.

MELCHIOR: Herr Zangler.

ZANGLER: *(Looking round)* Have you seen them yet?

MELCHIOR: Not yet, Herr Zangler.

ZANGLER: Remember—absolute discretion.

MELCHIOR: Yes, Herr Zangler.

ZANGLER: *(Looking round)* Don't draw attention to yourself—blend into the background.

MELCHIOR: Very good, Herr Zangler.

ZANGLER: Where the devil are you?

MELCHIOR: Here, Herr Zangler.

ZANGLER: Ah.

(MELCHIOR is evidently located behind the Chinese screen. He remains invisible. ZANGLER addresses himself to the screen.)

Now listen. I don't want any scandal. Just keep them under observation. We may have to assume a false identity.

MELCHIOR: Classic! I'll do a waiter—they're imported here, you know.

ZANGLER: What a pretentious place. Trust my niece.

MELCHIOR: Yes, I'll do one of my Italian waiters.

ZANGLER: *(Glancing round with disgust)* La dolce vita!—pah! Cognoscenti!—pooh! *(Furiously)* Prima donna!!

MELCHIOR: Quite good—put more of a shrug into it—cognosc*enti*—prima *donna*—!

(WAITER ONE enters to move the screen to one side of the room.)

WAITER ONE: Permettetemi signori di spostare questo paravento . . .[*Excuse me, gentlemen, may I just move this screen for you . . .*]

(As WAITER ONE smartly folds the screen shut, MELCHIOR's voice is cut off.)

MELCHIOR: Now that's a completely different—

(WAITER ONE moves the screen over to the door and leaves. ZANGLER follows anxiously and addresses the screen.)

ZANGLER: Are you all right?

(ZANGLER *opens up the screen and* MELCHIOR *now makes his
first appearance, limping into view, severely kinked.* ZANGLER
is relieved and at once drops the uncharacteristic solicitude.)
Honestly, I've never known such a buffoon! I'm going to
have to straighten you out when I get you home!

MELCHIOR: Thank you very much, Herr Zangler.

ZANGLER: Now go outside and have a look round.

(*Three* WAITERS *enter, one at a time, a few paces apart, from
the door leading to the restaurant. They cross the stage
briskly and exit through the swing door into the kitchen.*)
For all we know Sonders and Marie may have finished
their hors d'oeuvres and slipped away for the entrée.

MELCHIOR: No, sir, that's their coach outside.

ZANGLER: Is it? Where's the coachman?

MELCHIOR: In the kitchen having a quick one.

ZANGLER: Fetch him in here, I want to speak to him.

MELCHIOR: At once, Herr Zangler.

(*The first* WAITER *re-enters from the kitchen carrying a
veritable pagoda of crockery. He crosses briskly in the
direction of the restaurant.*)

ZANGLER: And remember what I said—no scandal—complete
discretion—

(*The second* WAITER *follows the first* WAITER *in a similar
manner.*)

MELCHIOR: Very good, Herr Zangler—

(MELCHIOR *turns and departs efficiently through the kitchen's
exit door. There is an impressive crash of falling crockery
beyond the door.* MELCHIOR *re-enters through the kitchen's
entrance door.*)
He's not there. (*He approaches the garden door.*) Hey you!
Coachman! You're wanted in here!

COACHMAN: (*Outside, shouts*) What do you want?

MELCHIOR: In here!

ZANGLER: (*Shouting discreetly*) Discretion, damn you!

MELCHIOR: (*Whispers to* ZANGLER) Sorry.

(*The* COACHMAN *enters from the garden. He is a large man,
immensely cloaked, wearing a tall hat; he carries a whip.*)
(*Discreetly*) Ah, coachman—my employer wishes to see
you—in private—it's a matter of some delicacy—we rely on

48

your discretion—you know what I mean?

COACHMAN: (*Roars*) Say no more, lead me to her. Where is she? (*He cracks his whip.*) If she's a goer, and has an arse a man can get a decent purchase on—

MELCHIOR: No, no!—

COACHMAN: (*Relatively quietly*) You're right!—discretion!—Tell her to meet me behind the stables.

MELCHIOR: No . . .

ZANGLER: You there!

COACHMAN: Who's that?

MELCHIOR: My employer.

(ZANGLER *comes forward importantly and halts.*)

ZANGLER: Zangler. Import and merchandising.

COACHMAN: (*Comes forward and clicks his heels*) Bodelheimer. Transport and waiting around.

ZANGLER: Purveyor of high-class provisions, supplier of cooked meats and delicacies to the gentry.

COACHMAN: Horse manure.

ZANGLER: How dare you!

COACHMAN: I supply horse manure.

ZANGLER: Oh, I see. Well, look here, Bodelheimer, I am a man of some consequence in the Grocers' Company. You'll do what I tell you if you know what's good for your business.

COACHMAN: Horse manure. (*Astutely*) And transport.

ZANGLER: Quite. Now. You have been engaged for the evening by a man who is escorting a certain young lady in a Scottish get-up.

(*The* COACHMAN *evidently has two personalities, one for sexual interests and the other for everything else. He drops the other.*)

COACHMAN: And what a corker! A pippin! She has a poise— a freshness—

ZANGLER: Quite—

COACHMAN: —an arse any man would give his eye teeth to sink into—

ZANGLER: That's quite enough.

COACHMAN: Happy the man who enjoys the freedom of her lacy bodice!

ZANGLER: (*Angrily*) You are addressing her guardian, sir!

49

COACHMAN: What are they like then?

ZANGLER: Will you be quiet!

COACHMAN: (*Quietly*) Sorry, what are they like?

ZANGLER: Now listen—

COACHMAN: Round like apples, or slightly pointy like pears?

ZANGLER: How dare you!

(*The* COACHMAN *lifts* ZANGLER *off his feet by his lapels.*)

COACHMAN: Answer me!

ZANGLER: (*Gasps*) Slightly pointy!

(*The* COACHMAN *throws him aside triumphantly.*)

COACHMAN: I knew it, by God!

(ZANGLER *reels over to* MELCHIOR.)

ZANGLER: Are you sure this is him?

COACHMAN: Conference or Williams?

ZANGLER: For God's sake, the man's obsessed!

(*But the* COACHMAN *pulls himself together suddenly and resumes his dignified personality.*)

COACHMAN: I'm sorry, your honour!—my apologies!—please disregard it. I'll be all right now.

ZANGLER: Are you quite sure?

COACHMAN: Oh yes. These attacks never last long.

ZANGLER: What sets you off?

COACHMAN: Thinking about buttocks, sir.

ZANGLER: Well, can't you keep your mind off them?

COACHMAN: I'm a coachman.

ZANGLER: Thank God we're back on the point. Now, when your passengers re-enter your coach, I want you to take them on a roundabout route to Twenty-three Carlstrasse.

COACHMAN: Where's that?

ZANGLER: Twenty-three Carlstrasse.

COACHMAN: I can't do that, they'll report me.

ZANGLER: The man is abducting my niece.

COACHMAN: Well, I don't know about that.

ZANGLER: I do. I'll go and fetch the constable and explain to him . . . (*He jingles his purse to make the point.*) He can jump up behind and persuade them to enter the house if they give you any trouble.

COACHMAN: It's out of the question.

ZANGLER: Here's one half your compensation. When you deliver the fugitives, Miss Blumenblatt will give you the other.

COACHMAN: Say no more! Is she a goer then?

ZANGLER: I will follow and have the man put on a charge, and thus avoid a public scandal. You go back to your place. As soon as they climb abroad, whip up your arse . . . No!

MELCHIOR: Stick up—

ZANGLER: No!

MELCHIOR: Horse—

ZANGLER: That's the boy. Whip up your horse and hand the fugitives personally to Miss Blumenblatt.

COACHMAN: Sporty type is she? Likes a good time?

ZANGLER: (*Incredulously*) She's fifty-seven!

COACHMAN: (*Losing interest*) Oh, well, look . . .

MELCHIOR: Or to her French maid.

COACHMAN: French maid? Will she let me in?

MELCHIOR: She's known for it.

(COACHMAN *turns to leave*.)

ZANGLER: (*To* MELCHIOR) I've heard remarks.

COACHMAN: What are they like?

ZANGLER: Slightly pointed.

(COACHMAN *exits*.)

How did you know about the French maid?

MELCHIOR: You mean there is one?

ZANGLER: I'll go and fetch a constable.

MELCHIOR: What about your celebration supper with your fiancée?

ZANGLER: Sonders has ruined my plans. I'll just have some cooked goose while I'm waiting to pickle his cucumber—no—some pickled cucumber while I'm waiting to cook his—

MELCHIOR: Got it.

(ZANGLER *leaves in the direction of the restaurant.* WAITER TWO *enters with a trolley bearing* ZANGLER's *celebration supper*.)

WAITER TWO: Here we are! One birthday supper for two as ordered. Lobster Thermidor, roast fowl, champagne and how many candles will she want on the cake?

MELCHIOR: Take that away. Snuff the candles and cancel the cake. Bring me some beer and pickles. I want the table over there, my master wants a clear view of the window.

WAITER TWO: What am I going to do with all this?

MELCHIOR: I am not a clairvoyant. Have you seen a young couple, the woman in a Scottish get-up?

WAITER TWO: What clan?

MELCHIOR: Machiavelli!

(WAITER TWO *leaves*. SONDERS *and* MARIE *enter*.)

MELCHIOR: It's them!

MARIE: Oh August, it's not proper.

SONDERS: Here is a paper proving you are of an age to be married without your guardian's consent.

MARIE: But it's not proper.

SONDERS: I assure you it is indistinguishable from the real thing. Keep it with you at all times.

(MELCHOIR *takes a napkin and menu from a table and confronts them boldly*.)

MELCHIOR: Buona sera!—you wisha da carta?

SONDERS: (*Fluently*) No, grazie tante; un bel cioccolato caldo ci aspetta alla nostra tavola in giardino, per me e per la mia amica. [*No thank you very much. My companion and I have some hot chocolate waiting for us at our table in the garden.*]

MELCHIOR: Right, squire . . . Sorry . . . I thought you were someone else.

(SONDERS *and* MARIE *exit*. GERMAN COUPLE *enter*.)

MELCHIOR: It's them!

(*The* GERMAN COUPLE *look at him with alarm and incomprehension.* MELCHIOR *addresses them with hearty innocence*.) Nothing! All clear! Take no notice! Carry on!

(*The* GERMAN COUPLE *ignore him*.)

(What weather we're having, eh! Turning out a bit dank. Is it cold outside?

GERMAN MAN: Bitte?

MELCHIOR: Is it? Last night was definitely dank. Would you say tonight was as dank or not as dank?

GERMAN WOMAN: (*Leaving*) Danke.

MELCHIOR: (*Amazed*) Danker?

GERMAN MAN: Bitte.

MELCHIOR: Please yourselves. Sparkling couple. I don't think it's them—all they can talk about is the weather.

(SCOTTISH COUPLE *enter*)

SCOTTISH MAN: Flora!

SCOTTISH WOMAN: Ye bluidy great loon, Hamish McGregor—

MELCHIOR: It's them!

SCOTTISH WOMAN: And to think we're missing Viennese Week in Fort William!

(SCOTTISH COUPLE *exeunt.* CHRISTOPHER *and* MME KNORR *enter, followed by* WEINBERL *and* MRS FISCHER. MELCHIOR *steps to one side.*)

MME KNORR: Ah, le beau monde!

MELCHIOR: It's them!

WEINBERL: Look, about us being married—

MRS FISCHER: I won't feel married until we've had the consommé.

MELCHIOR: Pretzels!

(MELCHIOR *exits through kitchen. Glass crash. He re-enters.*)
(*To Weinberl*) I don't care if you're married or not. You can do what you like!
(MELCHIOR *exits.*)

MME KNORR: What a strange fellow.

MRS FISCHER: That's never happened to me before at the Imperial Gardens Café.

WEINBERL: Yes, it's the first time for me, too.

CHRISTOPHER: It happens to me every time I come.

MRS FISCHER: We'll stay here, Eugenia, do you mind?

CHRISTOPHER: Well, I've reached the heights.

MRS FISCHER: The restaurant is so crowded and frankly I had no idea these Scottish patterns had become quite so common.

WEINBERL: I've got four guilders left after paying the coachman.

MME KNORR: It's the penalty of success, Hildegarde.

CHRISTOPHER: If only my mother could see me now!

MRS FISCHER: Unfortunately the success is yours, while the penalty is mine.

CHRISTOPHER: She never dreamed that one day I'd be rubbing shoulders with the crème caramel!

WEINBERL: Have you got any cash?

CHRISTOPHER: People of my class don't carry cash.

WEINBERL: I only had ten guilders when I set out.

CHRISTOPHER: Ten guilders! You hoped to acquire a past for ten guilders?

WEINBERL: Well I was single then—how was I to know I'd be married for dinner?

MME KNORR: (*Approaching*) Here we are. I'm hungry.

WEINBERL: (*To* CHRISTOPHER) You're not.

CHRISTOPHER: Sit down here, my Empress.—(*To* WEINBERL.) Not what?

MME KNORR: (*To* WEINBERL) Your cousin takes great liberties considering I'm engaged to be married.

CHRISTOPHER: Be mine tonight and I will reveal my true identity and give you half my kingdom.

WEINBERL: (*To* CHRISTOPHER) Not hungry.

CHRISTOPHER: (*Snaps at him*) Not even Herzegovina, but if you don't make the best of yourself you'll end up serving in a shop.

MRS FISCHER: (*Approaching*) Has the champagne arrived yet?

WEINBERL: I don't think we should eat here. It's all together too spartan for my taste.

MME KNORR: Don't blame me—it's the penalty of—

MRS FISCHER: Spartan!—I know it's not what you're used to but Madame Knorr and I don't know any better. Where's the Mumms?—I'm dying.

CHRISTOPHER: It's probably out the back.

WEINBERL: The service here is terrible. Waiter! You see? Let's move on.

MRS FISCHER: Don't be ridiculous. Anyway you let the coachman go—I don't know why you didn't ask him to wait.

WEINBERL: I didn't care for him. He seemed a very disagreeable fellow.

MRS FISCHER: That was because of your tip.

WEINBERL: I gave him a very good tip.

CHRISTOPHER: So did I.

WEINBERL: Ne'er cast a clout till May is out.

CHRISTOPHER: Get into cocoa at five per cent.

WEINBERL: Two very good tips.

MRS FISCHER: My husband likes to pretend he's parsimonious.

MME KNORR: You mean there's another one like him?

WEINBERL: Anyway I thought it would be nice to walk back across the park.

MRS FISCHER: Walk? Not b—

MME KNORR: There's a waiter—call him over.

WEINBERL: (*Feebly*) Waiter . . . waiter . . .

CHRISTOPHER: Waiter!

WAITER TWO: Coming, sir!

WEINBERL: (*To* CHRISTOPHER) Four guilders!

CHRISTOPHER: What?

WEINBERL: (*Bowing his head*) *Four guilders* our sins as we *four guilden* that trespass against us. (*He catches* MRS FISCHER'*s eye*.) Grace.

MRS FISCHER: Hildegarde.

WAITER TWO: Are you ready to order, sir?

WEINBERL: Ah, waiter!—sit down, my dear fellow. You strike me as being a splendid chap. What will you have?

WAITER TWO: Sir?

WEINBERL: Why should we accept the places allotted to us by an economic order that sets one man above another? I've been giving this matter a great deal of thought lately, and it seems to me that, in a nutshell, the value of labour capital—

MRS FISCHER: What are you babbling about?

WEINBERL: You may call it babble but one day, given its chance, Weinberlism will give birth to a new order. History is waiting.

MRS FISCHER: We are *all* waiting.

WAITER TWO: I wouldn't have the special—it's herring in oatmeal.

WEINBERL: Society's accounts will be settled once and for all, and when the bill comes, waiter, I want you to think of me as a comrade.

WAITER TWO: Yes, sir. And I wouldn't have the neeps either, if I were you.

WEINBERL: What are the neeps?

WAITER TWO: I wouldn't know, sir. That's why I wouldn't have them.

MRS FISCHER: Well, we'd like a drink to begin with.

WEINBERL: All right—bring us three beers and an extra glass.

MRS FISCHER: Such a sense of humour. He knows I never drink beer.

WEINBERL: Two beers and a glass of water.

MRS FISCHER: I must have something hot.

WEINBERL: Hot water.

MRS FISCHER: I mean something hot to eat.

WEINBERL: Two beers and a radish.

MME KNORR: You're right—he's hilarious.

MRS FISCHER: This has gone quite far enough.

WEINBERL: All right! Bring us two beers, two glasses of the house red and two sausages for the ladies.

MRS FISCHER: The house red?

WEINBERL: The wurst is yet to come.
(*Smartly to* CHRISTOPHER) Get it?

CHRISTOPHER: Got it.

WEINBERL: Good—that's all we got.
(WEINBERL *hands the menu to* WAITER TWO.)
My compliments to the official receiver.

MRS FISCHER: You obviously have no idea how to entertain a lady.

CHRISTOPHER: Watch this! (*He addresses* WAITER TWO *imperiously.*) You there—what's your name—we want the best dinner in the house, and we want it now!

WAITER TWO: Yes, sir! (*He clearly prefers* CHRISTOPHER's *type of customer. A thought strikes him.*) I happen to have a lobster just ready to serve.

CHRISTOPHER: Excellent.

WAITER TWO: Thermidor.

CHRISTOPHER: Excellent, Thermidor!

WAITER: And a roast fowl with all the trimmings, and for dessert . . . It's not anybody's birthday, by any chance?

MME KNORR: (*Amazed and pleased*) Yes! It's mine!

WAITER TWO: Gateau l'anniversaire—you get a bagpiper with that.

CHRISTOPHER: A bagpiper— good. We'll drink champagne to start, champagne with the main course and with the dessert we'll have some—

WEINBERL: (*Alarmed*) Champagne?

CHRISTOPHER: Trockenbeerenauslese. You think I know nothing?

WAITER TWO: An excellent choice, sir. And if I may say so, it is a pleasure to serve a gentleman. (*He glances meaningfully at* WEINBERL *and departs.*)

WEINBERL: It's people like him who are going to put a spoke into Weinberlist Theory. (*To* CHRISTOPHER.) Nevertheless the bill will come.

CHRISTOPHER: People of my class don't pay the bill.

WEINBERL: I mean—

CHRISTOPHER: (*Very deliberately*) I know what you mean. I am not entirely stupid. Society will pay. *Our* society. Do you follow me?

WEINBERL: Not exactly . . .

CHRISTOPHER: (*Expansively*) It's a damnable thing Weinberl, but when the reckoning comes the clever people are nowhere to be found. They've gorn . . . you see . . . disappeared . . . leaving the bill to be paid by the bourgeoisie . . . the shop-keepers . . . the widows . . . and such like, get me?

WEINBERL: (*At last*) Got you!

MRS FISCHER: Oh, do stop talking politics, we came here for a celebration dinner.

(WEINBERL's *manner has changed dramatically.*)

WEINBERL: My dear wife, why didn't you say you were hungry! We'll have a lobster *each*.

MME KNORR: Oh, it's true love.

WEINBERL: My Empress!

MRS FISCHER: (*Drily to* MADAME KNORR) Another one.

WEINBERL: I will give you half my kingdom, too!

MRS FISCHER: Hungary?

WEINBERL: Starving!

(*To* WAITER TWO *who has reappeared with the* ZANGLER *dinner trolley.*)

Ah, there you are at last—capital!—look sharp if you value your job, there's plenty of others'll do it for the money.

(MELCHIOR *enters from the garden with the other 'Italian'* WAITER ONE. *The situation is that the* WEINBERL *party have sat themselves down at the table stage left. The* ZANGLER *table is stage right, but both tables are quite near the centre.*)

MELCHIOR: What's all this?—I've arranged for my employer to eat here . . . and now these people have pushed in.

CHRISTOPHER: It's a free country.

MELCHIOR: Oh, classic!

CHRISTOPHER: It wasn't meant to be original.

WAITER ONE: (*Italian accent*) There's room for everybody.

(WAITER ONE *pours champagne.*)

MELCHIOR: My employer wishes to eat alone.

WEINBERL: Your employer seems to be confused about the nature of this establishment. It's what we call a restaurant.

MELCHIOR: Why don't you have your dinner somewhere else?

WEINBERL: Why don't you take yourself off before you get a lobster down your britches.

(WAITER TWO *is serving up dinner for four.*)

MELCHIOR: Please! My master wishes to have a clear view of that hansom cabman while he's eating.

WEINBERL: Your master's taste in cabmen is something we prefer not to discuss.

MELCHIOR: If only this stupid place had a dividing wall.

CHRISTOPHER: Perhaps your master should arrange to be preceded everywhere by a couple of rather fetching bricklayers.

WAITER ONE: (*Italian accent*) Signor, there is a Chinese screen which we use sometimes when a customer feels the drought —droot—draught.

MELCHIOR: That will have to do. Come here and help me with it.

MME KNORR: What a nuisance!

MRS FISCHER: (*Shudders*) Chinoiserie . . . and tartan . . .

CHRISTOPHER: Wait a minute! We can't be shown up like this in front of your wife and her friend.

(WEINBERL *and* CHRISTOPHER *get up and accost* MELCHIOR *and* WAITER ONE *who are bringing forward the screen.*)

WEINBERL: We don't intend to eat our dinner screened off from public view like a lot of—

CHRISTOPHER: Journalists—

WEINBERL: —So unless you want your Chinese screen folded round your ears—

MELCHIOR: I warn you, my master will not be put out for the likes of you.

WEINBERL: You may tell your master that if he has a bone to pick with me I don't wish to see his dog.

MELCHIOR: You can tell him yourself. I can hear him coming.

(*The sound of spurs approaching.* WEINBERL *and* CHRISTOPHER *speak together.*)

WEINBERL: ⎫
⎬ (*Levelly*) Screen.
CHRISTOPHER: ⎭

(WEINBERL *and* CHRISTOPHER *change tack with great*

smoothness and take the screen in hand, moving it so that it separates the two tables.)

MELCHIOR: Classic . . .

(ZANGLER *enters.* WEINBERL *and* CHRISTOPHER *sit down at their table visibly cowering.*)

ZANGLER: Melchior.

MELCHIOR: Your honour.

ZANGLER: Everything's arranged. The constable is poised to pursue Sonders. He's emptied my seal but his lips are pursed. No—he pursed to suppose—no—

MELCHIOR: Supper is served—

ZANGLER: No!—Oh, supper is served!

MELCHIOR: That's the boy.

(ZANGLER *sits down at his table.* WAITER ONE *sets out the beer and pickles and leaves.* WAITER TWO *wheels away the empty trolley.*)

ZANGLER: What is this screen doing here?

MELCHIOR: There's a very rough crowd at the next table—a couple of tarts and their night's work. I didn't want you to be disturbed.

ZANGLER: Good.

(*At the other table* WEINBERL *has poured the champagne. Supper commences.*)

MME KNORR: Well, life is full of surprises! I wish you all the luck in the world!

CHRISTOPHER: (*Quietly*) Thank you. We're going to need it.

MME KNORR: I mean the newly-weds.

CHRISTOPHER: (*Quietly*) Oh yes. (*To* WEINBERL.) All the luck in the world.

WEINBERL: (*Squeakily*) Thank you.

ZANGLER: (*To* MELCHIOR) Fetch me the paper and meanwhile go and keep an eye on Sonders and Marie.

(MELCHIOR *procures, at the side of the room, a newspaper on a pole which he hands to* ZANGLER.)

They're at a table in the garden. Let me know if he gets up.

MELCHIOR: I'll throw a bucket of water over them.

ZANGLER: No—no scandal!

MRS FISCHER: . . . And not forgetting *your* wedding plans, Eugenia . . . all the luck in the world! (*She toasts* MADAME

KNORR.)

MME KNORR: Thank you.

MRS FISCHER: Chink glasses.

(*They chink glasses.*)

CHRISTOPHER: (*Quietly*) All the luck in the world.

(CHRISTOPHER *chinks glasses with* MADAME KNORR.)

MME KNORR: Thank you. Chink glasses. (*To* WEINBERL.) Thank you.

(WEINBERL *is staring into space.* CHRISTOPHER *speaks quietly to* WEINBERL.)

CHRISTOPHER: Chink glasses.

WEINBERL: (*Squeakily*) Are they? They must go with the screen.

MRS FISCHER: Why are you speaking like that?

WEINBERL: (*Squeaks*) Like what?

MRS FISCHER: You're speaking in a peculiar way.

WEINBERL: (*To* CHRISTOPHER) Am I?

CHRISTOPHER: (*Quietly*) Not that I noticed.

MME KNORR: (*To* CHRISTOPHER) What's happened to your voice?

CHRISTOPHER: (*Quietly*) Nothing—there's no need to shout.

MME KNORR: I'm not shouting, I'm speaking normally.

WEINBERL: (*Squeaks*) Not so loud.

MRS FISCHER: And why aren't you eating?—lost your appetite?

CHRISTOPHER: (*Quietly to* WEINBERL) Chicken?

WEINBERL: (*Squeaks*) Wouldn't you be?

MME KNORR: I'd like some chicken. And some more champagne. I can feel it working already.

CHRISTOPHER: (*Quietly*) Breast or leg?

MME KNORR: All over.

CHRISTOPHER: (*Quietly to* WEINBERL) Breast or leg?

WEINBERL: (*Squeaks*) I'll take wing—have you got it?

CHRISTOPHER: (*Quietly*) Got it. (*To* MADAME KNORR.) The bottle's empty. I'll get a waiter.

(CHRISTOPHER *gets up and moves to the coatstand where, unnoticed by the women, he puts on* MRS FISCHER's *full-length tartan coat and puts the hood over his head.*)

WEINBERL: (*Squeaks*) I'll get one too.

MRS FISCHER: We don't need two waiters.

WEINBERL: (*Squeaks*) All right, I'll help him get the first one.

MRS FISCHER: Don't be silly—

MME KNORR: Oh, look—I've got the wish-bone!

WEINBERL: Have you?

MME KNORR: Come on, Hildegarde—

> (MADAME KNORR *and* MRS FISCHER *pull the wish-bone.*)
>
> Ah, well done! You've got the main part.

WEINBERL: (*Squeaks to* MADAME KNORR) That means it's your wish.

MME KNORR: No—it's your wife's wish.

WEINBERL: (*Squeaks*) That's not how we play it.

MRS FISCHER: I'm beginning to regret that I ever married you.

WEINBERL: You'd better both have a wish.

MME KNORR: Oh—all right—

WEINBERL: Close your eyes, count to twenty and don't tell me what you wish.

MME KNORR: ⎱
MRS FISCHER: ⎰ (*Together*) One–two–three–four–(*fade out*).

> (MADAME KNORR *and* MRS FISCHER *close their eyes.* CHRISTOPHER *has crept along the back wall into* ZANGLER's *area and leaves through the garden door.* ZANGLER *is distracted by his newspaper.*)

ZANGLER: (*Shakes his head sadly*) Viennese champion cabertosser fails to qualify at Braemar— (*Then puzzled*) What paper is this?

> (*Meanwhile* WEINBERL *has crept away up the stairs and is leaving by the gallery window in order to drop into the cab.*

MME KNORR: ⎱ (*Together*) . . . seventeen–eighteen–nineteen–
MRS FISCHER: ⎰ twenty.

MRS FISCHER: Good heavens! It works!

> (CONSTABLE *enters from garden.*)

CONSTABLE: Sir—a young couple have leapt into your coach.

ZANGLER: Did one of them look Scottish?

CONSTABLE: I don't know but the other one had a tartan cloak.

ZANGLER: It's them! Jump up behind and take them to Miss Blumenblatt's, Twenty-three Carlstrasse.

> (CONSTABLE *exits. Two* WAITERS *enter and move the screen.*)

WAITER ONE: Off with the lights.

> (*Enter* BUSBOY *with birthday cake, followed by* PIPER.)

ALL: (*Singing*) 'Happy birthday to you,
Happy birthday to you,

> Happy birthday dear Madame Knorr,
> Happy birthday to you.'

MME KNORR: Thank you.

WAITER ONE: Turn on the lights.

ZANGLER: My cake!

MME KNORR: Zangler!

ZANGLER: My fiancée!

(SONDERS *and* MARIE *enter.*)

SONDERS: My cab!

ZANGLER: Sonders!

SONDERS: My God!

MARIE: My uncle!

ZANGLER: My ward!

BUSBOY: (*To* ZANGLER) Your bill!

(ZANGLER *faints at the sight of it.*)

Living room, MISS BLUMENBLATT's *flat*
Double entrance doors, interior door, window to dark exterior, the bottom of a staircase, and another exit route which could be a chimney. Geraniums in pots. Candlesticks.

MISS BLUMENBLATT *is sitting reading the newspaper aloud to* LISETTE, *the French maid. She is twice interrupted by a* PARROT *in a cage; the* PARROT *says, 'Anything in the paper?', receives a glare of reproof from* MISS BLUMENBLATT, *and then the parrot says, 'Sorry', and* MISS BLUMENBLATT *reads from the paper:*

MISS BLUMENBLATT: '. . . In deploring these scenes of un-Austrian excess, we do not make the error of confusing café society with society in general. Yet the example of the Roman Empire lies ever before us. When those who presume to set standards are seen to have abandoned decent Aryan values for the degenerate postures of an alien culture, we say enough is enough. We have nothing against the Celtic race as such. We are assured that the Celts have a long and obscure history, and have made their contribution to science and the arts, such as it is. But their ways are not our ways, and we cannot but condemn this infatuation with the barbarian baroque universe of Sir Walter Scotch and his ilk. It is a moral issue . . .'

That's all very well, but it doesn't stop them advertising
Hunting-Stuart underdrawers in the same paper. Hardly
comme il faut.

LISETTE: Oui, Madame, 'ardly like he must. But 'ow late it is
for our guest not arriving.

MISS BLUMENBLATT: I can't think what has happened. My
brother-in-law's letter definitely said that he was sending
Marie to my safe keeping today. I was looking forward to
seeing the dear child again after these ten years. She will
find me more sympathique than Zangler has bargained
for. Her fate is just like my own. I too know what it is to
have loved and to have been separated from the man who
stole my heart . . .

LISETTE: Oh, Madame, 'ow I long for a man to steal mine!
'Ow will I know when it 'appens?

MISS BLUMENBLATT: You will know, never fear. With me it was
on a horse-tram in the Bahnhofstrasse . . . The chestnut
trees were in bloom . . . He sat down opposite me. Our
eyes met. I smiled.

LISETTE: What 'appened to 'im, Madame?

MISS BLUMENBLATT: He jumped off between stops and got
knocked down by a tram coming the other way. But it was
still love, and it was still separation. I'll never forget the
pain as he passed out of my view for ever!
(*Approaching sound of bawling.*)
Is that those people next door playing the bagpipes again?

LISETTE: I think it is a commotion outside. I will go to see.
(*She goes and immediately the* CONSTABLE *enters, driving*
WEINBERL *and* CHRISTOPHER *before him.* CHRISTOPHER *is still
dressed as a girl in the stolen Scottish cloak from the restaurant.
The cloak is very similar to the one worn by* MARIE.)

CONSTABLE: In you go and no arguments.

WEINBERL: Someone is going to pay for this.

CONSTABLE: What makes you think they haven't?

CHRISTOPHER: I'm not the woman you think I am. I'm not even
the woman you *think* is the woman you think I am.

MISS BLUMENBLATT: (*Rising to her feet*) To what am I owed this
scene of un-Austrian excess?
(*Screams off stage.* COACHMAN *enters with* LISETTE *over his*

shoulder showing her Scottish bloomers.)

Lisette!—déshabillé!

CONSTABLE: Hold your horses!

COACHMAN: (*Putting* LISETTE *down*) A thousand apologies . . .
please disregard . . . I'll be all right now. It's these cold
nights—the steam rising off their sleek rippling haunches.

LISETTE: Wait!

(LISETTE *kisses him firmly on the mouth.*)

At last!

COACHMAN: (*Highly gratified*) Are you a goer?

LISETTE: I am a goer! You have horses?

COACHMAN: I have the finest pair of chestnuts of any coachman
in the city!

(LISETTE *swoons in his arms.*)

(*Bewildered*) What did I say?

LISETTE: (*Reviving*) Tonight, my window will be open!

MISS BLUMENBLATT: Who are all these people? What are they
doing here?

CONSTABLE: My instructions are that this couple are to remain
here until the arrival of your brother-in-law.

MISS BLUMENBLATT: What? Surely this can't be the young woman?

WEINBERL: Of course she isn't—

CHRISTOPHER: And I can prove it.

WEINBERL: —if she has to. (*To* CHRISTOPHER) At the same time
we don't want to be taken for someone who leaves society
to pay his bills.

CONSTABLE: I have a letter here from your brother-in-law which
explains.

MISS BLUMENBLATT: Let me have it.

(CONSTABLE *hands her* ZANGLER'S *letter.*)

CONSTABLE: I'll station myself on the front steps, and wait for
your brother-in-law.

(CONSTABLE *exits*)

WEINBERL: Thank heavens! Now you can see that my friend
and I are the innocent victims of a police force the like of
which would explode the credibility of a comic opera.

(MISS BLUMENBLATT *finishes reading letter.*)

MISS BLUMENBLATT: (*Folding up the letter*) Ah—now I under-
stand.

64

WEINBERL: Thank goodness—

MISS BLUMENBLATT: Lisette . . . you know where we keep the tin of broken biscuits. Take the coachman into the kitchen and give him one.

LISETTE: Oui, Madame. Walk zis way.

(LISETTE *exits followed by the* COACHMAN.)

WEINBERL: We must be going—we have a long way to get home.

CHRISTOPHER: Yes, and somebody really ought to give us our fare for our trouble.

MISS BLUMENBLATT: (*Barring their way*) Stop! You are not leaving here.

WEINBERL: What!

CHRISTOPHER: It wasn't our fault. Don't blame us.

(MISS BLUMENBLATT *takes him into an embrace.*)

MISS BLUMENBLATT: My dear pretty child—of course I don't blame you! Your fate is exactly like my own. It happened to me on a horse-tram in the Bahnhofstrasse!

WEINBERL: You mean, the minute you got on it took off like a rocket—?

MISS BLUMENBLATT: I mean *love*! Oh, you have behaved recklessly but who can gainsay the power of love? And you, sir, you have much to answer for but do not give up hope. I am not the woman you think I am.

CHRISTOPHER: What? You don't mean—

WEINBERL: Of course she doesn't—Madame, would you mind telling us exactly what is in that letter?

MISS BLUMENBLATT: Only what you would expect a possessive guardian to write when his virgin niece has been abducted by a notorious Don Juan.

WEINBERL: He's as wrong about me as he is about her.

CHRISTOPHER: Wronger if anything.

MISS BLUMENBLATT: Of course he is. Have no fear. I will see you married in the morning.

WEINBERL: (*Without thinking*) Thank you. No—I think we ought to wait—she's so young, and I'd like to sleep on it, elsewhere—

(*The doorbell is heard.*)

MISS BLUMENBLATT: (*Shouts*) Lisette!

(*The kitchen door opens smartly and* LISETTE *appears,*

breathing heavily, her maid's cap back to front, the tartan ribbons falling over her face. She marches to the door.)
By the way did the Coachman take the biscuit?

LISETTE: He is taking it now, Madame. (*She opens the double doors and goes to the unseen front door.*)

MISS BLUMENBLATT: (*To* CHRISTOPHER) This may be your uncle.

CHRISTOPHER: None too soon.

WEINBERL: This'll clear things up.

(LISETTE *appears with* MELCHIOR.)

. . . on the other hand maybe it won't.

LISETTE: This man insists on being admitted. (*She continues towards the kitchen and leaves without ceremony.*)

MELCHIOR: Fraulein Blumenblatt!

MISS BLUMENBLATT: Well, sir?

(WEINBERL *and* CHRISTOPHER *are naturally surprised and dismayed.*)

CHRISTOPHER: That's—

WEINBERL: Zangler's servant!

MELCHIOR: My employer has sent me ahead to explain to you that this young couple who got into the coach are not actually the young couple (*He notices* WEINBERL *and* CHRISTOPHER) . . . It's them!

MISS BLUMENBLATT: Of course it's them!

MELCHIOR: Not only is it them, it's him!

MISS BLUMENBLATT: Do you know this man, Herr Sonders?

(WEINBERL *looks around in surprise and then realizes that he is being addressed.*)

WEINBERL: Sonders?

CHRISTOPHER: Marie's lover! She must think I'm—

MISS BLUMENBLATT: What's the matter, Marie?

CHRISTOPHER: (*Panicking faintly*) Oh, I've got it!

WEINBERL: (*Terrified*) I think I gave it to you.

MELCHIOR: Shame on you, sir!

MISS BLUMENBLATT: Don't be impertinent.

MELCHIOR: But this man is—

MISS BLUMENBLATT: I know all about that—

MELCHIOR: My employer was obliged to pay this man's bill.

MISS BLUMENBLATT: What bill?

MELCHIOR: To save the ladies from being turned over to the

police.

MISS BLUMENBLATT: What ladies?

MELCHIOR: And now he's got another one. (*To* CHRISTOPHER) Don't have dinner with him, miss!—he'll alter you before the dessert—no—he'll desert you before the altar.

MISS BLUMENBLATT: What is all this nonsense? Who sent you?

MELCHIOR: Your brother-in-law, Herr Zangler. He mistook this man for Sonders, and this lady for his niece—

WEINBERL: Exactly! So he wants you to let us go before he gets here—

MISS BLUMENBLATT: But that's the exact opposite of what it says in this letter. (*To* MELCHIOR) You're obviously not to be trusted.

(*The doorbell sounds again.*)

(*Shouts*) Lisette!

(LISETTE *enters in even more disarray and goes to open the door.*)

MELCHIOR: This must be Herr Zangler.

(LIGHTNING *whinnies offstage.*)

CHRISTOPHER: Lightning! . . . (*To* WEINBERL) Are you a goer?

WEINBERL: I am a goer!

(WEINBERL *starts to climb out of window when* LISETTE *re-enters.*)

LISETTE: Herr Weinberl is here.

(WEINBERL *has one leg over the windowsill. He pauses.*)

WEINBERL: Weinberl?

(WEINBERL *puts his leg back into the room.*)

MISS BLUMENBLATT: Herr Weinberl? Show him in. A thoroughly reliable man, I've heard Zangler speak of him.

WEINBERL: Have you?

MISS BLUMENBLATT: Don't concern yourself. You haven't a care in the world.

(LISETTE *reappears with* SONDERS.)

LISETTE: Herr Weinberl.

(LISETTE *makes a dignified but determined exit to the kitchen.* SONDERS *bows.*)

SONDERS: Madam, my apologies for calling so late. Weinberl.

MISS BLUMENBLATT: I'm delighted to make your acquaintance.

Let me introduce you to Herr Sonders.

(WEINBERL *and* SONDERS *scrutinize each other suspiciously.*)

Herr Sonders . . . Herr Weinberl.

Herr Weinberl . . . Herr Sonders.

But perhaps you two already know each other.

WEINBERL: (*Stiffly*) I don't believe I've had the honour.

SONDERS: No, I don't believe so.

(SONDERS *is very aware of* CHRISTOPHER *who is hiding his face in his hood.*)

(SONDERS *reaches for* CHRISTOPHER's *hand and kisses it.* MELCHIOR *is puzzled and mutters to himself.*)

MELCHIOR: Madam, it's him!

SONDERS: Marie and I must leave immediately. Herr Zangler has changed his mind and instructed me to take Marie away. Come on, my dear, your uncle is waiting for us—

MISS BLUMENBLATT: Just one moment, Herr Weinberl. Kindly desist from ordering people in and out of my house as if it were a blazing cuckoo-clock. Marie happens to be in love with Herr Sonders.

SONDERS: Well, yes and no—

MELCHIOR: Excuse me . . .

MISS BLUMENBLATT: (*Shouts*) Yes and no! The moment they met she was absolutely bowled over. It is something I can understand because her fate is precisely my own, except that in my case it was a horse-tram in the Bahnhofstrasse.

SONDERS: You were run over by a tram?

MELCHIOR: Madam . . .

MISS BLUMENBLATT: Furthermore one only has to look at Herr Sonders to see that he is no Don Juan. Look into his eyes. I have seen more treachery in a cocker spaniel.

(*She takes* WEINBERL *by the arm and turns aside to confer with him.*)

This is what we must do. I will send Zangler a message with this Weinberl to come here and . . .

(SONDERS *is making sidelong attempts to capture* CHRISTOPHER's *attention.* CHRISTOPHER *is cowering from the possibility.*)

SONDERS: Marie . . . Marie . . . Who is this impostor? How . . .?

(*Meanwhile* MELCHIOR *is scrutinizing* SONDERS *from closer range.*)

MELCHIOR: Madam . . . It's him!

SONDERS: How dare you!

MISS BLUMENBLATT: What . . .?

MELCHIOR: He is the real imposter!

SONDERS: What does this man want? Who are you?

MISS BLUMENBLATT: (*To* SONDERS) You mean you don't know
him? And he's been putting himself about as Zangler's
servant! I knew he wasn't to be trusted! (*Shouts*) Lisette!
(*The kitchen door crashes open,* LISETTE *sways in the doorway,
glazed, discreetly disarrayed, utterly changed, and goes to the
door.*)
Fetch the constable in here.
(LISETTE *passes through on the errand like a practised drunk.*)
(*To* MELCHIOR) I am having you arrested.

MELCHIOR: (*Aghast*) Me?

MISS BLUMENBLATT: For false impersonation.

MELCHIOR: This place is teeming with frauds! I am about the
only person here who isn't pretending to be somebody else!
(*The* CONSTABLE *enters.* LISETTE *remains outside.*)

CONSTABLE: What can I do for you, Ma'am?

MISS BLUMENBLATT: Apprehend this person.

MELCHIOR: Watch yourself, flatfoot.

CONSTABLE: 'Have a care, Constable.'

BLUMENBLATT: I mean arrest him.

SONDERS: Get rid of him.

WEINBERL: Yes, the man's a menace.
(LISETTE *now appears in the doorway.*)

LISETTE: Herr Zangler and party!

MISS BLUMENBLATT: Show him in.
(*In the moment between her announcement and* ZANGLER's
entry, SONDERS, WEINBERL *and* CHRISTOPHER *leave the room
by different routes but with identical timing.* WEINBERL
leaves by the window. CHRISTOPHER *goes up the stairs.*
SONDERS *leaves by the chimney, if possible.*
ZANGLER *comes in with* MADAME KNORR *and* MRS FISCHER *on
his arm and* MARIE *following.*
The CONSTABLE *pauses but still keeps hold of* MELCHIOR.
LISETTE, *without pause, goes straight back to the kitchen.*)

ZANGLER: Here we are, better late than never!

69

PARROT: Who's a pretty boy, then?

MELCHIOR: Oh, thank goodness—

ZANGLER: First things first. Let me introduce my fiancée and my fiancée's friend, Frau Fischer—Fräulein Blumenblatt . . .

MISS BLUMENBLATT: Enchantée.

ZANGLER: And this is my ward, Marie.

MISS BLUMENBLATT: Are you sure?

ZANGLER: The wedding is tomorrow.

MISS BLUMENBLATT: (*Looking round and noticing their absence*) What happened to Herr Sonders and . . .?

ZANGLER: Not *her* wedding—my wedding.

MISS BLUMENBLATT: Such haste?

ZANGLER: I'm not letting Madame Knorr out of my sight until we're married. I have my reasons. Why has the constable got my Melchior by the geraniums?

MISS BLUMENBLATT: You mean he's really—?

MELCHIOR: Oh, tell her who I am!

ZANGLER: He's my servant, of course.

(*The* CONSTABLE *releases* MELCHIOR.)

MELCHIOR: And do you have a salesman called Weinberl?

ZANGLER: I have.

MELCHIOR: Where is he now?

ZANGLER: At home fast asleep above the shop.

MELCHIOR: I rest my case.

MRS FISCHER: Weinberl! Wasn't that the name of—?

MME KNORR: It was! The one with the cousin who stole your coat!

MISS BLUMENBLATT: Not a tartan coat with a hood just like Marie's?

MRS FISCHER: Yes, I'm afraid it was.

ZANGLER: Surely it can't have been Weinberl.

MISS BLUMENBLATT: They were here!

MELCHIOR: I told you it wasn't Sonders.

MRS FISCHER: It was my so-called husband.

ZANGLER: Well, was he so-called or wasn't he? Where is he?

MISS BLUMENBLATT: He was here just now. And the window is open.

(ZANGLER *rushes to and through the window.*)

ZANGLER: My God, I was just about to make him my partner! If I find he's been on the razzle—

(MELCHIOR *is helping* ZANGLER *out through the window, and he follows.*)

MELCHIOR: (*Disappearing*) Classic!
  (*Sounds of* ZANGLER *and* MELCHIOR *rushing round the garden.* MADAME KNORR *watches from the window.*)

MME KNORR: (*Fondly*) Isn't he masterful? Did you notice the spurs?

MRS FISCHER: I think I prefer him to your first husband, Eugenia.

MME KNORR: Oh yes, *he* had two left feet, poor Alfred . . .

MISS BLUMENBLATT: What happened to him?

MME KNORR: He got knocked down by a horse-tram in the Bahnhofstrasse.
  (MISS BLUMENBLATT *faints.*)

MISS BLUMENBLATT's *garden*
A high wall running across the stage with a door set into it. The side of MISS BLUMENBLATT's *house. Door into house from garden. Upper bedroom window.*

ZANGLER *and* MELCHIOR *are, as it were, beating the bushes.*

ZANGLER: The garden is completely walled in and the gate is locked, but there's no sign of them. What's happened to the coachman?

MELCHIOR: He's very thick with the parlourmaid, apparently.

ZANGLER: Well, he's supposed to remain outside.

MELCHIOR: He didn't want to frighten the horses.

ZANGLER: Tell him to bring his coach round to the gate. If we set off now we'll be home by first light. Weinberl won't be expecting me back so early, I'll catch him on the hop. If it's the same Weinberl, he's finished in high-class groceries—I'll see to that.
  (LISETTE *enters the garden from the house in great excitement. Light spills from the open door.*)

LISETTE: Monsieur! One of the persons is fled to my room.

ZANGLER: Lock the door on him!

LISETTE: The person, he has locked it.

ZANGLER: Break it down!

LISETTE: I have another key.

71

(LISETTE, ZANGLER *and* MELCHIOR *pile back into the house,*
closing the door and leaving the garden dark again.
WEINBERL *comes out of hiding.*
Moonlight.)

WEINBERL: (*Whispering loudly*) Christopher!
(*He looks round vainly.* CHRISTOPHER *is at the upstairs*
window however.)

CHRISTOPHER: (*Whispering loudly*) Herr Weinberl!

WEINBERL: Is that you?

CHRISTOPHER: Yes!

WEINBERL: Where are you?

CHRISTOPHER: Here—and someone's trying to unlock the door!

WEINBERL: Can you get down?

CHRISTOPHER: No. Can you get over the wall?

WEINBERL: No. We're done for. I'm sorry, Christopher.

CHRISTOPHER: It wasn't your fault, Mr Weinberl. Thank you for
everything. It was a wonderful razzle.

WEINBERL: Yes. Not bad, really. To hell with them.

CHRISTOPHER: (*Urgently*) There's somebody coming behind you!
(WEINBERL *goes back into hiding.* SONDERS *approaches*
cautiously with a ladder. SONDERS, *looking around in the*
dark.)

SONDERS: (*Whispers*) Marie . . .

CHRISTOPHER: August! . . .
(SONDERS *looks up and sees him.*)

SONDERS: Marie! Courage, mon amour! I have a ladder!

CHRISTOPHER: (*Unwisely*) First class!

SONDERS: Is that really you?

CHRISTOPHER: (*Changing tack*) Oh, August, it's not proper!

SONDERS: It's you! Courage, my little cabbage—(*He puts the*
ladder up against the window.) Trust me!

CHRISTOPHER: I will, I will!
(CHRISTOPHER *comes down the ladder.*)

SONDERS: Have you got the documents?

CHRISTOPHER: What?

SONDERS: Have you got the documents?

CHRISTOPHER: What documents?

SONDERS: You can't have forgotten the documents I gave you in
the restaurant.

CHRISTOPHER: Oh those documents!

SONDERS: Well, where are they?

(CHRISTOPHER *points dramatically upwards.*)

I'll have to go and get them.

(SONDERS *climbs up.* LIGHTNING *whinnies off-stage.*)

CHRISTOPHER: Lightning!

(CHRISTOPHER *and* WEINBERL *take ladder to the wall. They
hear the coach approaching—they hide again behind the
summerhouse.*

The COACHMAN *climbs from his coach on to the wall and hears*
LISETTE *scream.*)

COACHMAN: Lisette! Oh, here's a ladder!

(COACHMAN *climbs down the ladder, takes it to the window
and climbs through, into* LISETTE's *bedroom where he loudly
encounters* SONDERS.

*At the same time the door from the house is flung open. It
releases, in a high state of excitement,* ZANGLER, MELCHIOR,
MADAME KNORR, MRS FISCHER, MARIE *and* MISS BLUMENBLATT.)

ZANGLER: There's a ladder! They've got away! Unlock the gate!

(MISS BLUMENBLATT *runs forward with a large key and
unlocks the gate in the wall.*)

Where's the coachman?

(*From the now darkened bedroom,* SONDERS, *wearing the*
COACHMAN's *hat and cloak, descends by the ladder.

Everybody else, except* MISS BLUMENBLATT, *who is holding the
gate open, is passing through the wall and straight into the
interior of the coach outside the gate.* MARIE *is last in the
queue.* SONDERS *removes the ladder from the window and
places it against the wall.*)

SONDERS: (*To* MARIE) Courage, my darling!

(MARIE *gasps and passes through into the coach.

SONDERS *goes up the ladder and takes the* COACHMAN's *seat.
Everybody is now inside the coach, which departs.

LIGHTNING *whinnies offstage.*)

CHRISTOPHER: Lightning!

(LIGHTNING *enters,* CHRISTOPHER *mounts up and* WEINBERL
leads them off.)

WEINBERL: Giddy up Lightning!

(*They exit.*)

ZANGLER's *shop*

WEINBERL *and* CHRISTOPHER *arrive on* LIGHTNING.

The coach is now seen through the panes of ZANGLER's *shop window.*
The occupants are all unpacking themselves from the interior.

SONDERS *gets down from the coach.*

ZANGLER, MADAME KNORR, MRS FISCHER, MARIE *and* MELCHIOR
disappear noisily from view and enter the ZANGLER *premises off*
stage. None of this is especially explicit. The stage is mainly occupied,
of course, by the empty interior of the shop. It is early morning and
the shop is not open yet.

WEINBERL *and* CHRISTOPHER *try the shop door from the outside,*
unsuccessfully. There is a desperation about them and they disappear
from view. Meanwhile, ZANGLER *has been heard from within shouting*
for WEINBERL.

ZANGLER: (*Offstage*) They're not upstairs— they're not
downstairs—if they're not in the shop we've got them!
(*The trap door in the floor opens and* CHRISTOPHER *emerges.*
He drops the trap door as ZANGLER *hurries into the shop.*
ZANGLER *is somewhat taken aback by seeing* CHRISTOPHER.)
Ah—it's you.

CHRISTOPHER: Good morning, Herr Zangler. (*He goes to the*
street door and starts unbolting it.) Just opening up, Herr
Zangler!

ZANGLER: Where's Weinberl?

CHRISTOPHER: He's here, Herr Zangler.

ZANGLER: Where?

CHRISTOPHER: Where?

ZANGLER: Yes, where?

CHRISTOPHER: You mean, where is he now, Herr Zangler?

ZANGLER: (*Impatiently*) Yes, yes—

CHRISTOPHER: Herr Weinberl—?

ZANGLER: *Yes!*—Where is Herr Weinberl now, you numskull!
(WEINBERL *plummets out of the chute and arrives behind the*
counter in a serving position.)

WEINBERL: Good morning, Herr Zangler.

ZANGLER: Shut up! Weinberl . . . My dear fellow . . . I
thought . . .
(*There is a general entry now. Firstly,* SONDERS *enters from*
the street door which has just been opened by CHRISTOPHER.

74

MARIE *enters from the house, followed by* MADAME KNORR,
MRS FISCHER *and* MELCHIOR.)

(*To* SONDERS.) What do you want? . . . Ah Marie . . . pay
the coachman from the till.

(MARIE *goes to the till and* SONDERS *goes to her.* ZANGLER's
attention turns to MADAME KNORR *and* MRS FISCHER. MRS
FISCHER *reacts to* WEINBERL's *presence behind the counter and
she approaches him so that only the counter is between them.
Meanwhile* MADAME KNORR *is taking in the presence of*
CHRISTOPHER.)

May I present my faithful partner, Herr Weinberl. We owe
him an apology, I feel . . . and my chief sales assistant,
Master Christopher . . . Madame Knorr . . . my fiancée,
the future Frau Zangler: the wedding is tomorrow.

CHRISTOPHER: Congratulations. Haven't we met before?

ZANGLER: What?

MME KNORR: No!

CHRISTOPHER: No, I thought not.

ZANGLER: Of course you haven't. This is the first time that
Madame Knorr has had the privilege of being swept round
the heap of my camp fire.

CHRISTOPHER: That's very well put Chief.

ZANGLER: I don't mean the heap of my camp fire.

CHRISTOPHER: Humped round the scene of your memoirs—

ZANGLER: No.

CHRISTOPHER: Squired round the hub of your empire.

ZANGLER: That's the boy—this is the first time Madame Knorr
has had the privilege of being squired round the hub of my
empire—What do you think of it all, Eugenia? Rather
empirical, eh?—Every modern convenience—a spring-
loaded cash flow to knock your eye out and your hat off!

(*He demonstrates the cash canister machine, which knocks*
SONDERS's *hat off.*)

Sonders!

SONDERS: Herr Zangler!

ZANGLER: I'll kill him!

MARIE: Oh, Uncle!

(*The* BELGIAN FOREIGNER *enters from the street, rather
dramatically.*)

FOREIGNER: Herr Sonders!
(*Everybody stops and gives him their attention.*)
SONDERS: Go away—for God's sake are you still dogging me for
a miserable unpaid hat-bill?
FOREIGNER: Herr Sonders! I am coming from Brussels. I am
coming from the lawyer of your relatively departed ant.
SONDERS: What?
FOREIGNER: Alas, your ant is mortified!
SONDERS: Mortified?
FOREIGNER: As a door nail.
SONDERS: My aunt! How dreadful! You mean my dear auntie in
Brussels has unfortunately passed away?
FOREIGNER: (*Pointing to* SONDERS) This man is too rich!
MARIE: Oh, oh darling, does this mean . . .?
SONDERS: (*To* ZANGLER.) Sir . . .
ZANGLER: Juan, isn't it?—
SONDERS: August.
ZANGLER: August, of course! . . . my dears . . . (*To* FOREIGNER.)
How much exactly . . .? Well, never mind for now—I
think we all deserve a champagne breakfast. Entrez tout le
monde! (*Shouts*) Gertrud! Bubbly all round!
(GERTRUD *enters.*)
Where have you been?
GERTRUD: Fetching the post.
ZANGLER: Jereboams! Bollinger!
GERTRUD: You're upset. I can tell.
ZANGLER: Get out and catch the pox—no—
GERTRUD: Pack my bags—
ZANGLER: No.
GERTRUD: Pop the corks—
ZANGLER: That's the boy—get out and pop the corks.
(GERTRUD *exits.*)
We have two happy couples to toast. After all, Marie is of
mortgageable age and August—(?)— (SONDERS *nods.*) August
here is a credit. To his profession. What are you in, by the
way?
SONDERS: Risk capital, mainly, I think, Uncle.
ZANGLER: Have you thought about high-class provisions?
SONDERS: We'll open an account as soon as we're married.

ZANGLER: Open an account? Tush, man, come in with me and you'll eat wholesale for the rest of your life! And that's another thing, August . . . (*piously*) I haven't got long . . .

SONDERS: (*Briskly*) We ought to be going too.

ZANGLER: One day, August, the Zangler empire will need a new hand in the till—no.

SONDERS: On the tiller.

ZANGLER: That's my boy!

(GERTRUD *enters with tray*.)

ZANGLER: Ah!—let the first glass be for the one who has entered my life and changed my fortune.

(*Gives first glass to* FOREIGNER *and then to* SONDERS *and* MME KNORR. GERTRUD *carries tray down the line*.)

ZANGLER: Marie . . . Frau Fischer . . . my faithful partner, Herr Weinberl.

GERTRUD: (*To* WEINBERL) There's a letter for you, Herr Weinberl.

(*She gives* WEINBERL *a letter which is of interest to* MRS FISCHER.)

ZANGLER: . . . and my Chief Sales Assistant, Christopher. I give you the Grocers' Company!

ALL: The Grocers' Company!

ZANGLER: You can be a victualler too, Julie.

SONDERS: August!

ZANGLER: August! . . . You can have my old uniform.

GERTRUD: (*To* WEINBERL) Old uniform—why you crafty old. . . .

ZANGLER: What is it?

GERTRUD: Twenty-three Carlstrasse. Miss Blumenblatt's.

ZANGLER: Where have you been?

(GERTRUD *exits*.)

ZANGLER: Herr Weinberl . . . would you escort Frau Fischer? You might become better acquainted.

MRS FISCHER: I am already well acquainted with Herr Weinberl.

ZANGLER: You are?

WEINBERL: You're not, are you?

MRS FISCHER: How can you say that after writing me all those romantic letters, Scaramouche!

WEINBERL: Elegant and Under Forty!

ZANGLER: Well! *Three* happy couples to toast, I believe!

(*Enter* GERTRUD.)

GERTRUD: Breakfast is served.

ZANGLER: Thank you Gertrud.

(*He starts to lead everybody out,*
MRS FISCHER *bringing up the rear.*)—Eugenia—

SONDERS: Marie.

WEINBERL: May I take you in Hildegarde?

MRS FISCHER: You've been taking me in for months, Herr
Weinberl.

(MRS FISCHER *exits.* WEINBERL *and* CHRISTOPHER *embrace with*
(*premature*) *relief.*

ZANGLER: (*Outside*) Melchior!

(WEINBERL *and* CHRISTOPHER *simultaneously realize that they*
could still be undone.)

WEINBERL: Melchior!

(*But* MELCHIOR *approaches with champagne bottle, recharges*
WEINBERL'*s and* CHRISTOPHER'*s glasses, produces a third glass*
from his pocket, fills it, and toasts them.)

MELCHIOR: Classic!

(MELCHIOR *goes out.*
WEINBERL *and* CHRISTOPHER *go to their places behind the*
counter. They drink a silent toast. They look at each other.)

CHRISTOPHER: (*As* WEINBERL) 'I don't think you know my wife!'

(WEINBERL *splutters with pleasure.*)

WEINBERL: (*As* CHRISTOPHER) 'We want the best dinner in the
house and we want it now!'

(*They splutter joyfully and pummel each other about the*
shoulders.)

CHRISTOPHER: (*As* MISS BLUMENBLATT) 'Herr Weinberl—Herr
Sonders—Herr Sonders, Herr Weinberl . . .'

WEINBERL: (*As* SONDERS) 'Marie—who is this impostor?'

(*But their joy evaporates almost immediately.* WEINBERL *sighs*
and reaches for the broom.)

Well . . . my chief sales assistant . . . Would you do me the
honour . . .

(*He bows and offers the broom which* CHRISTOPHER *takes.*)

The street door opens to admit a small RAGAMUFFIN.)

RAGAMUFFIN: Are you the grocer, your eminence?

WEINBERL I believe I am, sir.

RAGAMUFFIN: I understand you have an opening for an apprenticeship in the grocery trade.

WEINBERL: I believe I have, sir. The successful applicant will receive a thorough training in grocery, green grocery, charcuterie, weights and measures, stock-taking, window-dressing, debit, credit and personal hygiene. The hours are from dawn to dark and the pay is six guilders per month, less four guilders for board and lodging, one guilder for laundry, and one guilder put aside in your name against clothing and breakages. Would that be satisfactory?

RAGAMUFFIN: Yes, sir. I think that would be satisfactory.

WEINBERL: Have you any commercial experience?

RAGAMUFFIN: I have been chiefly holding horses' heads outside the Dog and Duck, sir. But I am my own master and can leave at any time.

WEINBERL: Christopher! Give him the broom!

RAGAMUFFIN: (*Joyfully*) Oh—thank you, sir!

(CHRISTOPHER *gives him the broom.*)

WEINBERL: You will find me a stern master but a fair one. I think I have some reputation in the mercantile world for—

(*Outside there is a roar of 'Weinberl' from* ZANGLER.)

(*Pause, gravely.*) Excuse me. I was away in Vienna yesterday and there are matters to discuss with my partner. (*He leaves.*)

RAGAMUFFIN: Vienna! Have you ever been to Vienna, sir?

CHRISTOPHER: Me? Oh yes. Good Lord. Of course.

RAGAMUFFIN: What is it like, sir?

CHRISTOPHER: (*Carelessly*) Vienna? Well it's . . .

(*Coming clean*) wonderful!

(*The* RAGAMUFFIN *sweeps with furious delight.* CHRISTOPHER *watches him.*)

PERSONAL PROPS

CUSTOMER
German newspaper & coin

MISS BLUMENBLATT
Spectacles (W)

CONSTABLE
Truncheon
'Scribble' letter (white paper)
White envelope addressed to—
    Miss Blumenblatt,
    23 Carlstrasse, Vienna

SONDERS
Document (pink ribboned)
Coin
Note pad for message in "zinger"

LADY IN BLACK
Cigar (slim panatella)
Matches—cigar type—*in* black bag

BELGIUM FOREIGNER
Spectacles (W)

MELCHIOR
2 fat cigars—punctured at smoking end
Testimonial (writing clear) folded in four
Matches—small, non-safety—in right hand waistcoat
    pocket

GERTRUD
Scissors on chatelaine
Brown duster

ZANGLER
Spectacles (W)
Pocket watch (W)

(W)—Wardrobe

Large gold coin – give to dresser & spare on DS.L. props
  table

LISETTE
Bunch of keys
Spectacles (W)

WEINBERL
'Scribble' letter (blue paper)
Blue envelope
3 or 4 stamps in leather wallet
Spectacles (W)

CHRISTOPHER
Duster – in apron

SECOND PROPS LIST

1:2

p DL watch. . . . . ward
Tray + duster, jug of ink, fresh blotting paper, fake
   flowers, p HB scissors on chatelaine. . . . ward
Coat hanger + old costume
2 prs. boots, boot clip at top

1:3 On Zangler's desk from C/U:

Cigars in box, matchlighter, vase, handbell, blotter,
   pens, inkwell, paper envelopes
Cash box + coins & paper money. In top left drawer
   of desk.
Belgian man's case + document
Tailor's dummy + new costume
Sweet jar of soft sweets
p JC pins, tape measure, bill
p BMc pencil
p MK testimonial, cigars in case, matches
p DL coins, pince nez

1:4

Sack of beans with schnapps bottle lying in top
Heavy unopened sack from cellar
2 schnapps glasses
2 lunchpacks wrapped in newspaper
Pretzels on stand. 1 per perf.
Whisk.
Worsted stocking + coins
Jar of rollmops ?
Written letter, blank envelope
Ink, pen, blotter
Large sweet jar of candy sticks
p RB wallet + stamps

1:5

Wooden sign 'Boy Wanted'

1:6

Nothing yet

1:7

Very sturdy bouquet
Gas key on pole
Beer mug
Cigarettes and matches in baccy tin

1:8

Label on cape
Indoor watering can
p RMc notebook & pencil

2:1

2 dirty coffee cups and saucers
12 napkins
2 liqueur glasses
4 table cloths
4 knives, forks, bread knife, soup spoon (dessert
  forks) *minimum*
8 wine lists
8 menus
2 empty trays
2 trays fixed dirty dishes
5 trays fixed food to be served
Tray + dish of fake lobster thermidor, & dish of fake
  chicken
Tray + beer & pickles for 2
Very large tray + lobster thermidor served on 4 plates,
  & dish of chicken. Lobster & upstage part of chicken
  is eaten.
4 plates same size as above
Plate of radishes
4 champagne glasses
Bottle of champagne opened every night
Ice bucket + ice
Floor stand for ice bucket
3 small vases of flowers
Basket of flowers

Tureen to go on MK's head
Newspaper on frame
Long coach whip
p birth certificate BMc

2:2

Sewing for Lisette
Newspaper with part of text
Large magnifier
Bottle of schnapps + glass
Letter opened, but no essential text
Cover over parrot cage

2:3

Binoculars
Ladder

2:4

Case from act one for Belgian
Plain white postcards
Letter left from 1:4
2 bottles of champagne. At least one opened each perf.
8 champagne glasses on tray
Duster
Sack for Weinberl to slide down chute. . . . very slippy
Coins in till
Whisk for 1:4
Wooden sign from 1:5

SKIN DEEP
Jon Lonoff

Comedy / 2m, 2f / Interior Unit Set

In *Skin Deep*, a large, lovable, lonely-heart, named Maureen Mulligan, gives romance one last shot on a blind-date with sweet awkward Joseph Spinelli; she's learned to pepper her speech with jokes to hide insecurities about her weight and appearance, while he's almost dangerously forthright, saying everything that comes to his mind. They both know they're perfect for each other, and in time they come to admit it.

They were set up on the date by Maureen's sister Sheila and her husband Squire, who are having problems of their own: Sheila undergoes a non-stop series of cosmetic surgeries to hang onto the attractive and much-desired Squire, who may or may not have long ago held designs on Maureen, who introduced him to Sheila. With Maureen particularly vulnerable to both hurting and being hurt, the time is ripe for all these unspoken issues to bubble to the surface.

"Warm-hearted comedy … the laughter was literally show-stopping. A winning play, with enough good-humored laughs and sentiment to keep you smiling from beginning to end."
– *TalkinBroadway.com*

"It's a little Paddy Chayefsky, a lot Neil Simon and a quick-witted, intelligent voyage into the not-so-tranquil seas of middle-aged love and dating. The dialogue is crackling and hilarious; the plot simple but well-turned; the characters endearing and quirky; and lurking beneath the merriment is so much heartache that you'll stand up and cheer when the unlikely couple makes it to the inevitable final clinch."
– *NYTheatreWorld.Com*

COCKEYED
William Missouri Downs

Comedy / 3m, 1f / Unit Set

Phil, an average nice guy, is madly in love with the beautiful Sophia. The only problem is that she's unaware of his existence. He tries to introduce himself but she looks right through him. When Phil discovers Sophia has a glass eye, he thinks that might be the problem, but soon realizes that she really can't see him. Perhaps he is caught in a philosophical hyperspace or dualistic reality or perhaps beautiful women are just unaware of nice guys. Armed only with a B.A. in philosophy, Phil sets out to prove his existence and win Sophia's heart. This fast moving farce is the winner of the HotCity Theatre's GreenHouse New Play Festival. The St. Louis Post-Dispatch called Cockeyed a clever romantic comedy, Talkin' Broadway called it "hilarious," while Playback Magazine said that it was "fresh and invigorating."

Winner!
of the HotCity Theatre GreenHouse New Play Festival

"Rocking with laughter...hilarious...polished and engaging work draws heavily on the age-old conventions of farce: improbable situations, exaggerated characters, amazing coincidences, absurd misunderstandings, people hiding in closets and barely missing each other as they run in and out of doors...full of comic momentum as Cockeyed hurtles toward its conclusion."
–Talkin' Broadway

TREASURE ISLAND
Ken Ludwig

All Groups / Adventure / 10m, 1f (doubling) / Areas
Based on the masterful adventure novel by Robert Louis Stevenson, *Treasure Island* is a stunning yarn of piracy on the tropical seas. It begins at an inn on the Devon coast of England in 1775 and quickly becomes an unforgettable tale of treachery and mayhem featuring a host of legendary swashbucklers including the dangerous Billy Bones (played unforgettably in the movies by Lionel Barrymore), the sinister two-timing Israel Hands, the brassy woman pirate Anne Bonney, and the hideous form of evil incarnate, Blind Pew. At the center of it all are Jim Hawkins, a 14-year-old boy who longs for adventure, and the infamous Long John Silver, who is a complex study of good and evil, perhaps the most famous hero-villain of all time. Silver is an unscrupulous buccaneer-rogue whose greedy quest for gold, coupled with his affection for Jim, cannot help but win the heart of every soul who has ever longed for romance, treasure and adventure.

THE OFFICE PLAYS
Two full length plays by Adam Bock

THE RECEPTIONIST
Comedy / 2m, 2f / Interior

At the start of a typical day in the Northeast Office, Beverly deals effortlessly with ringing phones and her colleague's romantic troubles. But the appearance of a charming rep from the Central Office disrupts the friendly routine. And as the true nature of the company's business becomes apparent, The Receptionist raises disquieting, provocative questions about the consequences of complicity with evil.

"...Mr. Bock's poisoned Post-it note of a play."
– New York Times

"Bock's intense initial focus on the routine goes to the heart of *The Receptionist's* pointed, painfully timely allegory... elliptical, provocative play..."
– Time Out New York

THE THUGS
Comedy / 2m, 6f / Interior

The Obie Award winning dark comedy about work, thunder and the mysterious things that are happening on the 9th floor of a big law firm. When a group of temps try to discover the secrets that lurk in the hidden crevices of their workplace, they realize they would rather believe in gossip and rumors than face dangerous realities.

"Bock starts you off giggling, but leaves you with a chill."
– Time Out New York

"... a delightfully paranoid little nightmare that is both more chillingly realistic and pointedly absurd than anything John Grisham ever dreamed up."
– New York Times

SAMUELFRENCH.COM

NO SEX PLEASE, WE'RE BRITISH
Anthony Marriott and Alistair Foot

Farce / 7 m, 3 f / Interior

A young bride who lives above a bank with her husband who is the assistant manager, innocently sends a mail order off for some Scandinavian glassware. What comes is Scandinavian pornography. The plot revolves around what is to be done with the veritable floods of pornography, photographs, books, films and eventually girls that threaten to engulf this happy couple. The matter is considerably complicated by the man's mother, his boss, a visiting bank inspector, a police superintendent and a muddled friend who does everything wrong in his reluctant efforts to set everything right, all of which works up to a hilarious ending of closed or slamming doors. This farce ran in London over eight years and also delighted Broadway audiences.

"Titillating and topical."
– NBC TV

"A really funny Broadway show."
– ABC TV

ANON
Kate Robin

Drama / 2m, 12f / Area

Anon. follows two couples as they cope with sexual addiction. Trip and Allison are young and healthy, but he's more interested in his abnormally large porn collection than in her. While they begin to work through both of their own sexual and relationship hang-ups, Trip's parents are stuck in the roles they've been carving out for years in their dysfunctional marriage. In between scenes with these four characters, 10 different women, members of a support group for those involved with individuals with sex addiction issues, tell their stories in monologues that are alternately funny and harrowing..

In addition to Anon., Robin's play What They Have was also commissioned by South Coast Repertory. Her plays have also been developed at Manhattan Theater Club, Playwrights Horizons, New York Theatre Workshop, The Eugene O'Neill Theater Center's National Playwrights Conference, JAW/West at Portland Center Stage and Ensemble Studio Theatre. Television and film credits include "Six Feet Under" (writer/supervising producer) and "Coming Soon." Robin received the 2003 Princess Grace Statuette for playwriting and is an alumna of New Dramatists.

WHITE BUFFALO
Don Zolidis

Drama / 3m, 2f (plus chorus)/ Unit Set

Based on actual events, WHITE BUFFALO tells the story of the miracle birth of a white buffalo calf on a small farm in southern Wisconsin. When Carol Gelling discovers that one of the buffalo on her farm is born white in color, she thinks nothing more of it than a curiosity. Soon, however, she learns that this is the fulfillment of an ancient prophecy believed by the Sioux to bring peace on earth and unity to all mankind. Her little farm is quickly overwhelmed with religious pilgrims, bringing her into contact with a culture and faith that is wholly unfamiliar to her. When a mysterious businessman offers to buy the calf for two million dollars, Carol is thrown into doubt about whether to profit from the religious beliefs of others or to keep true to a spirituality she knows nothing about.

CPSIA information can be obtained
at www.ICGtesting.com
Printed in the USA
BVHW050906230323
661004BV00012B/338

9 780573 620003